D0240094

# MRS BEETON
# CHICKEN,
## OTHER BIRDS
## & GAME

DOWNLOADED FROM

Mrs Beeton How to Cook

Mrs Beeton Soups & Sides

Mrs Beeton Fish & Seafood

Mrs Beeton Chicken, Other Birds & Game

Mrs Beeton Classic Meat Dishes

Mrs Beeton Cakes & Bakes

Mrs Beeton Puddings

BAINTE DEN STOC

WITHDRAWN FROM
DÚN LAOGHAIRE-RATHDOWN COUNTY
LIBRARY STOCK

# MRS BEETON CHICKEN, OTHER BIRDS & GAME

## ISABELLA BEETON & GERARD BAKER

### FOREWORD BY VALENTINE WARNER

*For my grandmothers Nora Baker and Elsie Hinch,*
*who spanned the gap between Isabella and me.*

Gerard Baker

This edition published in Great Britain in 2012 by Weidenfeld & Nicolson
Originally published in 2011 by Weidenfeld & Nicolson as part of *Mrs Beeton How to Cook*

1 3 5 7 9 10 8 6 4 2

Text copyright © Weidenfeld & Nicolson 2012
Design and layout copyright © Weidenfeld & Nicolson 2012

Design & Art Direction by Julyan Bayes
Photography by Andrew Hayes-Watkins
Illustration by Bold & Noble. Additional illustration by Carol Kearns
Food Styling by Sammy-Jo Squire
Prop Styling by Giuliana Casarotti
Edited by Zelda Turner

All rights reserved. No part of this publication may be reproduced, stored or transmitted, in any form, or by any means, electronic, mechanical, photocopying, recording or otherwise, without the prior permission of both the copyright owner and the above publisher.

The right of the copyright holder to be identified as the author of this work has been asserted in accordance with the Copyright, Designs and Patents Act 1988.

A CIP catalogue record for this book is available from the British Library.
ISBN 978 0 297 86682 4

The Orion Publishing Group's policy is to use papers that are natural, renewable and recyclable products and made from wood grown in sustainable forests. The logging and manufacturing processes are expected to conform to the environmental regulations of the country of origin.

Printed and bound in Spain

Weidenfeld & Nicolson
The Orion Publishing Group Ltd
Orion House
5 Upper St Martin's Lane
London WC2H 9EA

An Hachette UK Company

www.orionbooks.co.uk

# CONTENTS

| DUN LAOGHAIRE-RATHDOWN LIBRARIES | |
|---|---|
| DLR20001008910 | |
| BERTRAMS | 07/11/2012 |
| | £9.99 |
| EA | |

# FOREWORD

On my shelves, bending under the weight of many cookbooks, is my great grandmother's copy of Mrs Beeton; a heavy, red-bound edition, the broken spine covered in reams of crispy old Sellotape, testament to the consulting fingertips of three generations of Nangle women. As a child I was fascinated by this book, primarily for its illustrations, as I sat on the stairs flicking through the colour plates, trying to find the calf's head, brown roasts and cuts of meat, upside down game birds and mad fancy salads.

Later on it was the bizarre recipe names that caught my interest, such things as curried toast or shrivelled oysters, kidney soup and baked tench. Both in images and text I had never come across these strange things: 'What did devils have to do with sardines?'

So much of my later food education came full circle back to Mrs Beeton. The book was a kind of serendipitous priming for the many things I like to prepare and eat now. It's a sanctuary for my occasionally cooked-out brain. Still today, when wandering through the pages, old ways are offered up alongside ideas of food for different environments – always something new or unknown. For all its old fashioned-ness the book remains strangely refreshing among modern day offerings that often lack logic or sense. It is a riveting catalogue that, thanks to Gerard Baker's work in this new edition, stands the test of time with a confidence that requires no simultaneous television series.

Despite a squeamishness that has crept into current British cookery, game sales are steadily rising and Mrs Beeton's ideas have been sensibly condensed to this collection of delicious and achievable recipes, little prompting needed with the tempting photography inside. Duck, venison, rabbit: these are important dishes, delicious tastes from the wild places – things of our land for the very people that live in it. A polished-off plate of hare, an empty glass, a ruddy cheek, a treat!

I fly the apron high for Mrs Beeton and feel that if she were leafing through this latest publication with a cup of tea and floured hands she would smile reflectively and close the book gently, happy that her good work had been upheld.

Valentine Warner

# THE INIMITABLE MRS BEETON

When Isabella Beeton first published *Beeton's Book of Household Management* in 1861, Britain was changing from a rural society, in which large numbers of people were involved in farming and many grew their own fruit and vegetables at home, to an industrialised one, where the development of modern transport networks, refrigeration and kitchen appliances brought a world of food to our fingertips.

Today, most of us have an image of Mrs Beeton as a matronly figure – brisk, efficient and experienced in the kitchen. In fact, Isabella Beeton was young and recently married, juggling working outside the home with running her household and coping with the demands of a husband and young family. Having worked on it throughout her early twenties, she saw her book published at the age of 25 and died just three years later.

Although she wrote of housekeepers, butlers and valets, her semi-detached in Hatch End was a world away from the big country houses of the preceding century, and although it is likely that she had some help in the kitchen, she almost certainly managed her home and most of the cooking herself. Her book was inspired by an awareness of the challenges faced by women like herself – and with that in mind, she used her position as editor of *The Englishwoman's Domestic Magazine* to pull together the best recipes and advice from a wide range of sources.

She was among the first revolutionary food writers to style recipes in the format that we are familiar with today, setting out clear lists of ingredients and details of time taken, average cost and portions produced (this last being entirely her invention). She also offered notes on how to source the best food for her recipes – placing particular emphasis on such old-fashioned (or, in our eyes, surprisingly modern) ideas as the use of seasonal, local produce and the importance of animal welfare.

It is easy to see why Mrs Beeton's core themes – buy well, cook well and eat well – are as relevant today as they were 150 years ago. Her original book was written with an awareness of household economy that we can take lessons from too. Because we have access to so much so easily, we often forget to consider how to get the most out of each ingredient – yet maximising flavour and nutrient value and minimising waste is as relevant in the twenty-first century as it was in 1861.

## The right ingredients

Mrs Beeton's original recipes have needed careful adaptation. In some cases, the modern recipes are amalgamations of more than one Beeton recipe or suggestion, which I hope give a more coherent whole. Many of the ingredients that may seem at first glance universal are so different today from those varieties Isabella would have been familiar with that using them in the original way can give quite different results to those intended. For those reasons, quantities needed to be not only converted but checked and altered. And all those cases where Mrs Beeton advised adding salt or sugar or honey or spices 'to taste' have been pinned down in real quantities, always keeping in mind both flavour and authenticity.

Cooking methods, too, were in some cases not replicable and in others simply no longer the best way of achieving the desired results. A significant factor in this is that the domestic oven was in its infancy in 1861, and Mrs Beeton was not able to make full use of it in her book. Most kitchens would instead have been equipped with old-fashioned ranges, and there is much mention of setting things before the fire, turning and basting. Baking or roasting, which we now consider simple processes, required constant attention 150 years ago. Oven temperatures, therefore, have all had to be deduced from a mixture of reading between the lines, comparing modern recipes, and testing, testing, testing.

The end result, however, has been to produce dishes that Mrs Beeton would, hopefully, have been happy to call her own.

## The legacy

After Isabella Beeton died early in 1865, her book took on a life of its own. It was endlessly enlarged, modern recipes were added and eventually, in the many, many editions of the book that have been published in the past 150 years, the spirit of the original was lost.

The picture of British food that Isabella painted in the first edition was about to change wholesale, and her book was destined to change with it. The aim of this collection is to reverse those changes: to return to real, wholesome, traditional British food, which Mrs Beeton might be proud to recognise as her own – and to put to rest the matronly image.

# INTRODUCTION

From roast haunch of venison (page 27) to a simple and satisfying game terrine (page 57), the variety of dishes in this book is guaranteed to open up your repertoire to a range of rich, flavourful, gamy tastes. Alongside the new, you'll find Mrs Beeton's take on old favourites (such as the perfect roast chicken on page 16), and adaptable base recipes for stocks and sauces. Traditional preparation techniques and butchery skills that would have been taken for granted 150 years ago are made practical and achievable.

The main difference between poultry and game is that poultry is farmed and available all year round. Game can be either reared or wild, and for everything other than farmed venison there are fixed seasons when it may be hunted (see page 88).

If you have never tried the many game birds and wildfowl (ducks and geese) available in this country, do so as soon as you can. They are truly delicious, a healthy source of protein, and most can be bought easily from butchers or supermarkets during the winter months.

Game birds divide roughly into those reared for shooting and those that are truly wild. Game birds that are reared – usually the pheasant, French (red-legged) partridge and, occasionally, the mallard – can be shot in a variety of ways. At one end of the scale is the small, country shoot, which usually consists of groups of friends meeting on farmland to shoot birds for their own consumption. Any excess may be sold to game dealers, but generally the numbers shot are in the dozens rather than the hundreds. At the other extreme is the large, formal driven-game shoot. This is where birds, such as pheasant and partridge, are 'driven' out of cover by a row of beaters with dogs to a line of standing guns. These shoots take place on farms and country estates and may bring down many thousands of birds during a season. The landowner sometimes sells the birds on to game dealers or directly to the public. However, there is a risk, when hundreds of birds are shot in a single day, that supply will exceed demand and many will go to waste.

Conservation plays a large part in a shoot. The types of birds targeted are often restricted so that, for example, only male birds may be shot later in the season. Wild birds that are not common, such as the English (grey) partridge, are usually left alone. Very large shoots must be managed carefully to limit their impact on local wildlife, and, sadly, this often does not happen. As an alternative to rearing game for shooting, an increasing number of estates manage habitats to encourage wild game birds to breed on their land. This is usually done with birds that are not reared and is particularly the case with red grouse.

# Cooking Techniques

It is important that chicken and turkey are cooked through. All game, however, can be eaten rare or medium, which ensures it remains tender. Thoroughly cooked game will be dry unless it is braised for several hours – for example in the venison casserole (see page 36).

## Frying

This method is suitable for the breast of game birds and venison, hare or rabbit loin. Trim the meat of any silver skin, sinew or fat then season with salt and freshly ground black pepper. Brown the pieces on all sides in a roomy frying pan over a medium-high heat, usually in oil or clarified butter. Don't crowd too much meat into the pan or it will steam and not fry.

## Braising

This moist, slow method suits older game birds, shoulder of venison or hare legs. Brown the meat first then add the vegetables and liquid and cook, covered, over a low heat or in a low oven.

## Roasting

A rapid method of cooking that suits all poultry and game birds, and joints of venison loin and haunch. Small birds roast very quickly, usually in less than 30 minutes, and so need to be browned in oil and butter before they go into the oven to enhance the flavour and add colour.

## Pot roasting

This is a useful way of cooking game, especially with older animals. Joints of venison or whole birds can be browned and then roasted in a covered pot with aromatics, vegetables and a small amount of stock to prevent the meat drying out.

## Hanging game

To develop the fullest flavour and improve tenderness, all game can benefit from being hung for a week in a cool and airy place. It must be hung under such conditions as soon as possible after being shot because in damp or warm weather it will deteriorate quickly and may attract flies or pests.

## Preparing meat

Knowing how to joint your meat is good for kitchen economy as it is invariably cheaper to buy a whole bird, or a whole rabbit (or hare), than it is to buy all the pieces separately. It is a doddle to do – and you are then also left with the carcass/neck and head, which can be used to make stock. The main requirement here is a good-quality cook's knife with a really sharp edge.

### Jointing a bird

Birds can all be jointed in the same way. First, place the bird breast side up. To remove a leg, first cut through the skin where the thigh joins the body to reveal the joint. Bend the leg back until the joint pops out of its socket. Holding the bone out of the way, cut through the tendons to detach the leg from the backbone. Repeat with the other leg. To detach the wings and to separate the thigh from the drumstick simply bend the joints backwards in the same way and cut neatly around the bone.

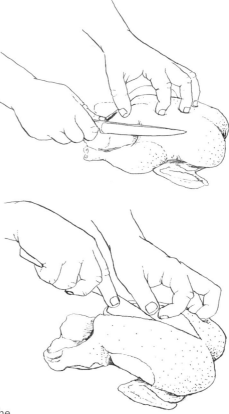

Finally, remove the breasts. Feel for the raised bony ridge of the breastbone and insert the full length of your knife to one side of it. Cut down until you feel resistance, then turn your knife out away from the breastbone and continue to slice around and underneath the breast, staying as close to the carcass as possible. Repeat on the other side.

### Jointing a rabbit or hare

To joint a rabbit or hare, lay it on a chopping board with the hind legs towards you. Make a cut across the pelvis just above the hind legs, and then cut each leg off, keeping your knife close to the bone. Twist the legs to free the joint.
Then, remove the forelegs, keeping your knife close to the rib cage. Cut the thin belly flaps off, ribs and all, and discard – the ribs are sharp so be careful. Finally, cut the saddle into two even parts.

## Carving birds

To carve a bird, first cut down in between the leg and breast, pushing the leg outwards with the knife to reveal the joint and then slicing through it to remove the leg. Separate the drumstick from the thigh by cutting through the elbow joint. Now that the breast is exposed, you can easily carve the meat into long, even slices. Alternatively, remove the breast as a whole piece in the same way as you would when jointing a raw bird (see page 12) and slice it into long even slices on a board. Repeat the same process on the second side.

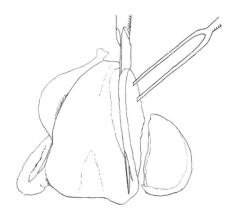

'Here is a grand dish for a knight of the carving knife to exercise his skill upon, and what will be pleasant for many to know is that there is but little difficulty in the performance.'

*Beeton's Book of Household Management*

## Resting meat

After roasting any meat it is important to rest it in a warm place. During cooking, moisture is pushed away from the hot surface of the meat and retained in the cooler centre. During resting, the heat equalises and the juices are reabsorbed. This means that less juices are lost when the meat is carved, leaving it more succulent. The length of time that meat should be rested for varies according to its size. Each recipe in this book gives an indication of the resting time needed.

Because the centre of the meat continues to heat up during the resting time, it is necessary to remove it from the oven before the serving temperature has been reached. If you test the meat after resting and find that it has not reached the required temperature, put it back into the oven for 5 minutes per 500g initial weight and then retest.

ROASTING

# ROAST CHICKEN

✳ Serves 4 ✳ Preparation time 5 minutes ✳ Cooking time 1 hour plus 20 minutes resting time

Mrs Beeton gives a nice recipe for roast fowl or chicken, and many for using up the leftovers. If you are using a larger or smaller chicken, calculate the cooking time at 20 minutes per 500g. Cook at 200°C/gas mark 6 for the first 25 minutes, and then lower the temperature to 150°C/gas mark 2 for the remainder of the cooking time.

**1.5kg whole chicken**

**15g softened unsalted butter**

**½ small, unwaxed lemon**

**small bunch thyme**

**1 bay leaf**

**salt and freshly ground black pepper**

special equipment

**a roasting tin and a temperature probe**

Preheat the oven to 200°C/gas mark 6.

Rub the chicken all over with the butter. Put the lemon, thyme and bay leaf inside the cavity of the bird, and then season the outside with salt and a few grindings of pepper. Place the bird in a roasting tin.

Roast for 25 minutes, then turn the oven down to 150°C/gas mark 2 for a further 30–35 minutes until a probe inserted into the thickest part of breast reads 65°C and into the thigh reads 70°C. Otherwise pierce the thigh with a skewer. If the juices run clear and are not pink, the chicken is cooked. If it is not quite cooked, leave it in the oven for another 10 minutes, and then retest.

Remove from the oven and cover loosely with foil. Leave the chicken to rest for 20 minutes in a warm place before carving and serving.

# ROAST & BRAISED TURKEY

✳ Serves 12 ✳ Preparation time 30 minutes
✳ Cooking time 3 hours for legs, 2 hours 15 minutes for crown including resting time

This dish takes its inspiration from Mrs Beeton's roast turkey, but since it is difficult to roast a large bird evenly, the legs of the turkey are braised slowly to soften them, and to give a wonderful gravy. The crown is then roasted to a perfect moistness without the worry that the legs will be underdone. Ask your butcher to remove the bird's legs and trim the backbone to neaten the crown. The wings can also be cut to the first joint and put in with the legs and giblets. The legs can be cooked the day before you roast the crown, which gives you a head start on your gravy if you are making this for Christmas lunch. Alternatively, if you have two ovens, they can be cooked simultaneously.

### for the braise

legs and wings from a
6.5kg turkey

giblets from turkey

1 carrot, peeled and cut
into large chunks

1 onion, peeled and
roughly chopped

1 stick celery, roughly
chopped

2 bay leaves

small bunch thyme

100ml dry white wine

800ml dark chicken stock
(see page 67)

salt and freshly ground
black pepper

### for the crown

3kg crown, trimmed,
at room temperature

25g salted butter

### for the gravy

15g unsalted butter

15g plain flour

600ml stock from the
braised legs

### special equipment

2 large roasting tins and a
temperature probe

Preheat the oven to 220°C/gas mark 7.

Season the legs well with salt. Place them in a roasting tin with the wings and cook for 15 minutes. Add the giblets and cook for another 15 minutes.

Remove from the oven and pour away any excess fat then add the vegetables, bay leaves and thyme and a few grindings of black pepper. Pour in the wine and stock. Cover the tin with a layer of greaseproof paper, and then a layer of foil. Turn the oven down to 150°C/gas mark 2 and return the roasting tin to the oven.

After 2½ hours remove the tin from the oven and pour off the liquid (you should have at least 600ml) into a large bowl. Allow it to cool, then skim off any fat. Discard the giblets, herbs and vegetables, but if you are preparing the legs ahead of time, wrap them in foil and chill.

To cook the crown, preheat the oven to 200°C/gas mark 6. Rub the butter all over the skin of the crown and season with 1 tsp salt and a few grindings of pepper. Set it on a roasting tin and place in the oven. After 30 minutes turn the oven down to 160°C/gas mark 3 for a further 1 hour 15 minutes.

(If the legs need reheating, return them to a roasting tin and pour over the stock. Place in the oven underneath the crown and allow to cook for 1 hour until they reach at least 73°C.)

To check the crown for doneness, insert a probe into the thickest part of the breast, right down to the bone. It should read at least 65°C. If not, leave the crown in the oven for a further 20 minutes and retest.

Remove from the oven and cover with a sheet of foil and several tea towels. Allow it to rest in a warm place for 30 minutes, by which time the heat at the thickest part will have reached at least 73°C.

To make the gravy, heat the butter in a saucepan over medium heat and stir in the flour. Let it bubble and when the mixture smells nutty and begins to turn brown add the stock from the legs a little at a time and cook, stirring, until you have smooth gravy. Boil for 3–4 minutes then season to taste and strain into a warmed sauceboat.

To serve, slice the meat from the legs and arrange at one end of a large serving dish. Place the crown alongside and take to the table. For notes on carving, see page 13.

**Note:** You should always ask for giblets when buying a turkey, as they are a valuable source of flavour. Inspect them carefully and cut away any dark green parts – these are contaminated with bile and will make your stock bitter.

# ROAST GOOSE

✳ Serves 6-8 ✳ Preparation time 5 minutes ✳ Cooking time 4 hours 15 minutes including resting time

To ensure a more even roast, Mrs Beeton's typical sage, onion and breadcrumb stuffing is cooked here alongside the bird. Mrs Beeton serves this dish with apple sauce (see page 76).

5kg whole goose

for the gravy

giblets from the goose, checked over and any green gall stains removed

2 shallots, peeled and roughly chopped

1 tbsp sunflower oil

100ml white wine

800ml dark chicken stock (see page 67)

1 large thyme sprig

1 bay leaf

15g unsalted butter

15g plain flour

for the stuffing

40g salted butter

300g onions, peeled and finely chopped

10 sage leaves, finely chopped

140g fresh white breadcrumbs

1 medium egg, beaten

salt and freshly ground black pepper

special equipment

2 roasting tins

Preheat the oven to 220°C/gas mark 7. Place the giblets and the shallots in a roasting tin, pour over the oil and toss to coat. Sprinkle the goose with salt and set in another roasting tin. Place the tin containing the giblets on the bottom oven shelf, and the goose on the shelf above. After 30 minutes, remove the giblets and turn down the temperature to 150°C/gas mark 2. Set the timer for 2 hours.

Transfer the roasted giblets and shallots to a medium saucepan. Add the white wine, stock, thyme and bay leaf and simmer gently for 2 hours. After this time, remove the goose from the oven, pour off any excess fat from the tin and cover with foil. Turn the oven down to 140°C/gas mark 1 and return the goose to the oven for a final 1½ hours.

Now make the stuffing. Melt the butter in a saucepan over a medium heat. Add the onions and a pinch of salt and cook, stirring, for 5-7 minutes, until the onions are soft, but not brown. Remove from the heat and stir in the sage leaves and the breadcrumbs. Add the beaten egg, mixing it in well. Season and transfer to a baking dish. Cover with foil and bake alongside the goose for 30 minutes, then take off the foil and allow the stuffing to brown in the oven for another 15 minutes. Remove the stuffing from the oven and keep warm.

Remove the goose from the oven and place on a warmed serving dish. Cover with foil and then a towel and leave to rest. For the gravy, melt the butter in a saucepan and stir in the flour. Let it bubble and, when the mixture smells nutty and begins to turn brown, add the stock a little at a time and cook, stirring, until you have a smooth gravy. Boil for 3-4 minutes, then season and strain into a warmed sauceboat.

# ROAST WILD DUCK

✳ Serves 4 ✳ Preparation time 10 minutes ✳ Cooking time 45 minutes including resting time

Mrs Beeton recommends serving a piquant accompaniment to roast duck, and her raspberry vinegar (see page 84) livens up the simple gravy perfectly. Serve this dish with steamed and buttered kale. This recipe can also be made with red grouse, in which case cook the birds for 20–25 minutes.

2 wild ducks, weighing around 1.3kg in total

1 tbsp sunflower oil

30g butter

300g red onions, peeled and very finely sliced

50ml red wine

150ml dark chicken or jellied game stock (see page 67 or 68)

1 tbsp raisins

2 tbsp raspberry vinegar (see page 84) or sherry vinegar

salt and freshly ground black pepper

special equipment

a roasting tin

Preheat the oven to 200°C/gas mark 6.

Season the ducks inside with salt and black pepper. Place the oil and 10g of the butter in a large frying pan over a medium to high heat. Add the ducks and brown them on all sides. Transfer the ducks to a roasting tin and place in the oven for 25 minutes.

Meanwhile, turn the heat under the pan to low and add another 10g of butter. Place the sliced onions and a pinch of salt in the pan. Once they begin to brown, add the wine and simmer until it has reduced to almost nothing. Then add the stock and raisins, stirring until the onions are soft and there is very little liquid left. Remove the pan from the heat and stir in the remaining 10g of butter and the raspberry vinegar.

Once the duck is cooked, cover it with foil and allow it to rest for 15 minutes in a warm place. Remove each breast in one piece and cut into 3 or 4 long slices. Drizzle some raspberry vinegar over each portion and serve with onions on the side.

**Note:** A bird shot in September will be fat from the late summer corn. A bird shot later in the season will be less fat but have a deeper flavour. Either bird would benefit from being roasted.

# ROAST PARTRIDGES

✳ Serves 4 ✳ Preparation time 25 minutes ✳ Cooking time 35–40 minutes including resting time

This is a simple yet mouth-watering way of cooking partridges. Serve them with a potato and cream gratin, and roast chicory with cooked pears (see *Mrs Beeton Soups & Sides*).

4 oven-ready partridges

2 tbsp sunflower oil

60g unsalted butter

2 shallots, peeled and finely chopped

4 large thyme sprigs

2 tbsp brandy or cognac

salt and freshly ground black pepper

special equipment

a large roasting tin and a temperature probe

Preheat the oven to 200°C/gas mark 6.

Place a large frying pan over a medium to high heat and add the oil and 15g of the butter. When it sizzles, add the birds and fry them on all sides for 5 minutes, or until they are a golden brown.

Divide the shallots, thyme and the remaining butter between the body cavities of the birds and put all the birds into a roomy roasting tin. Season with salt and pepper and pour ½ tbsp brandy into the body cavity of each bird.

Roast for 15 minutes for rare or 20–25 minutes for medium to well done, then remove from the oven and place on a serving dish in a warm place. Cover with foil and leave for 10 minutes. A temperature probe pushed into cooked and rested birds at the thickest part of the breast just above the wing joint should read 55°C for medium rare.

# POT-ROAST PHEASANT WITH CELERY

✳ Serves 4 ✳ Preparation time 15 minutes ✳ Cooking time 1 hour including resting time

Pheasants can be abundant in rural areas in the winter, and butchers often sell them very cheaply indeed, making them accessible to us in a way they would not have been to Mrs Beeton. She roasted her pheasant, but this updated one-pot recipe prevents the birds from drying out and provides a no-hassle gravy. The combination of pheasant with celery is a classic English pairing. If you can find it, use white blanched celery. Mrs Beeton would have been familiar with this, and it has the finest flavour. Any leftover legs can be used for the pheasant and chestnut soup (see page 70).

1 pheasant brace
(a 1kg cock and a 600g hen)

2 thyme sprigs

1 tbsp sunflower oil

50g unsalted butter

6 shallots, halved

4 sticks white blanched
celery, cut into 5cm lengths

2 carrots, peeled and cut into
3cm lengths

1 bay leaf

300ml dry white wine

150ml dark chicken or jellied game
stock (see page 67 or 68)

4 very thin rashers
dry-cure streaky bacon

2 tbsp finely chopped
celery leaves, to garnish

special equipment

a large flameproof casserole
with a lid and a temperature probe

Preheat oven to 160°C/gas mark 3.

Insert a sprig of thyme into the cavity of each bird.

Place a large casserole on a medium to high heat. Add the oil and half the butter and when it sizzles, add the birds and fry them until they are well coloured on all sides. Remove to a large plate. Add the vegetables to the casserole and fry until well browned. Then add the bay leaf, wine and stock.

When the liquid is simmering, return the birds to the casserole, grind some black pepper over them and lay the bacon over the birds. Cover with a lid and place in the oven for 20 minutes. For medium or medium-rare, the hen should be ready in 20 minutes, the cock in 30 minutes. A temperature probe inserted into the breast just above the wing joint should read 45–50°C. If you like your birds well done, cook for a further 10 minutes until the breasts are firm.

Once the birds are done remove the pot from the oven and put it in a warm place to rest with the lid on for 15 minutes. Then carve the breasts from the carcass and cut each one into 2–3 pieces. Place on a platter alongside the vegetables and sprinkle the finely chopped celery leaves over. The sauce should simply be skimmed to remove any fat, poured into a sauceboat and served alongside.

# WOODCOCK ON TOAST

✳ Serves 4 ✳ Preparation time 15 minutes ✳ Cooking time 12–15 minutes plus 10 minutes resting time

Woodcock make an excellent quick meal or shooting breakfast. Serve with a good bottle of Claret for a real treat. Small birds have traditionally been served on toast or buttered breadcrumbs to absorb the juices, as Mrs Beeton recommended doing with larks.

2 tbsp sunflower oil

60g unsalted butter

4 woodcock (see note below)

2 shallots, peeled and finely chopped

4 large thyme sprigs

2 tbsp brandy or cognac

salt and freshly ground black pepper

to serve

200ml dark chicken or jellied game stock (see page 67 or 68)

4 slices good bread

salted butter, for spreading

special equipment

a large roasting tin and a temperature probe

Preheat the oven to 200°C/gas mark 6. Heat a large frying pan over a medium to high heat, add the oil and a knob of the butter and, when it sizzles, add the birds. Fry them on all sides for 5 minutes, or until they are a mid-brown colour.

Place some shallot, a sprig of thyme and a small knob of butter into the body cavity of each bird and arrange them in a roomy roasting tin. Season with salt and black pepper and pour ½ tbsp brandy into the cavity of each bird.

Place in the oven. After 12 minutes remove the tin from the oven and transfer the birds to a serving dish. Set it in a warm place, cover with foil and leave for 10 minutes. After this time a temperature probe pushed into the thickest part of the breast should read 55°C for medium rare.

Meanwhile add the stock to the roasting tin and mix to combine with the cooking juices. Simmer to reduce for a quick gravy. Toast the slices of bread and spread with salted butter. Place each woodcock on a piece of toast and serve with the gravy on the side.

**Note:** Woodcock are traditionally cooked with their innards intact. If you cook the woodcock intact, you will need to remove the innards with a teaspoon after cooking. Discard the small, hard, round gizzard and the tiny, dark green gall bladder which is attached to the liver. Melt 10g butter in a small saucepan with a little garlic, fry for a minute or two and then add the innards and 1 tbsp brandy. Flame and mash the mixture with a fork as it cooks. Spread onto the toast and top with the woodcock.

# ROAST HAUNCH OF VENISON

✳ Serves 4 ✳ Preparation time 15 minutes ✳ Cooking time 30–40 minutes

A full hind leg (haunch) of roe deer will feed 6–8 people. A leg of red deer would be more likely to feed 10–12, but you are unlikely to be able to fit a whole haunch of that size into a domestic oven. Should you want to cook one, get your butcher to remove the shinbone and tie the leg to form an even shape. Allow 15 minutes per 500g for medium rare, following the method below, but leave the cooked meat to rest for at least an hour. This recipe assumes you are feeding a smaller number, in which case you should ask your butcher to tie you a boned joint from the top of the leg.

1 tbsp duck fat or sunflower oil

800g–1kg tied joint of venison

20g unsalted butter

2 shallots, peeled and
finely chopped

1 large thyme sprig

1 bay leaf

1 tsp juniper berries, crushed

½ tbsp sherry vinegar

200ml dark chicken or jellied game
stock (see page 67 or 68)

salt and freshly ground
black pepper

special equipment

a roasting tin

Preheat the oven to 160°C/gas mark 3.

Heat a large frying pan over a medium to high heat and add the duck fat or sunflower oil. Season the meat with a little salt and black pepper and add it to the pan. Fry it for 10 minutes, or until it is a deep, dark brown colour on all sides. Remove the pan from the heat.

Transfer the meat to a roasting tin and place in the oven. After 20–25 minutes, test with a temperature probe to see if the internal temperature has reached 50°C. If not, leave in the oven for a few more minutes and test again. When the meat is ready, remove it from the oven and place it on a serving plate. Cover it with foil and leave it in a warm place for 15–20 minutes.

Meanwhile, place half the butter in the frying pan over a low heat and add the shallots. Fry gently until the shallots soften and brown at the edges. Strip the leaves from the thyme sprig and add them to the pan, along with the bay leaf, juniper berries, vinegar and stock. Cook until it reduces to a syrupy sauce.

Stir in the remainder of the butter and the strain the sauce into a warm sauceboat. Carve the venison into even slices and serve with the sauce and a selection of seasonal vegetables.

SLOW
COOKING

# BRAISED HARE LEGS & SHOULDERS

✳ Serves 4 ✳ Preparation time 20 minutes ✳ Cooking time 3 hours

Mrs Beeton cooked young hares, called leverets, in butter and stewed older animals in a ragout or braise. Here, the traditional vegetable accompaniments of onions, carrot and celery have been added to the braise to give a fully flavoured sauce. Only use the legs and shoulders, which in any case will easily feed four. The saddle is best cooked separately and saved for a special dinner when there are just two of you (see page 46).

40g unsalted butter

legs and shoulders from a 2kg hare, weighing about 900g

350ml light red wine

100g streaky dry-cure bacon, diced

1 onion, peeled and finely chopped

1 small carrot, peeled and cut into small chunks

1 stick celery, finely chopped

1 garlic clove, peeled and halved

1 small rosemary sprig

small bunch thyme

2 bay leaves

400ml dark chicken stock (see page 67)

salt and freshly ground black pepper

special equipment

a roasting dish

Preheat the oven to 140°C/gas mark 1.

Place a heavy-bottomed pan over a medium to high heat, and add 20g of the butter until hot and foaming. Season the legs with a large pinch of salt, add them to the pan and brown well all over. This should take about 10 minutes.

Transfer the meat into a snug-fitting roasting dish and discard any fat from the pan. Now pour a little of the red wine into the pan and stir to dissolve any sediment. Pour this over the hare, then wipe out the pan and add the bacon. Cook the bacon, stirring, over a medium heat until it is golden.

Add the onion, carrot and celery and cook until softened and lightly brown. Add the garlic, herbs and a grinding of pepper and cook for 2 minutes. Add the rest of the wine and cook until completely reduced and beginning to caramelise. Add the stock, bring the mixture to a boil and pour it over the legs.

Cover the roasting dish closely with non-stick baking paper, then seal with a layer of foil. Place in the oven for 2½ hours, until the veg are tender and the meat is falling off the bone, then strain the liquid into a small pan placed on a high heat. Boil to reduce by half and then taste for seasoning.

Meanwhile, pick the meat from the bones in large chunks. Return to the pan with the reduced sauce and reheat to serve. Serve with mashed potatoes and a seasonal vegetable.

# CHICKEN BRAISE WITH MUSHROOMS

✳ Serves 4 ✳ Preparation time 15 minutes ✳ Cooking time 35 minutes

A quick way to cook a slowly reared chicken. Today's best equivalent would be an organic bird. Mrs Beeton's original recipe called for gravy, but you can use good chicken stock. Combined with the vegetables, the stock makes the dish rich and satisfying.

2kg whole chicken

3–4 tbsp sunflower oil

4 large field mushrooms, chopped into large chunks

1 onion, peeled and cut into large chunks

1 carrot, peeled and cut into 2cm chunks

2 garlic cloves, peeled

small bunch thyme

1 bay leaf

300ml light chicken stock (see page 66)

100ml double cream (optional)

salt and freshly ground black pepper

special equipment

a flameproof casserole or a large saucepan

Cut the chicken into pieces. Remove the legs and separate the drumsticks from the thighs, then cut each breast into two equal chunks. Season all over with a little salt.

Heat 3 tbsp oil in a large frying pan over a medium heat. Add the chicken pieces and fry until golden brown on all sides. Set aside the breast pieces and place the leg pieces into a flameproof casserole dish or large saucepan.

Turn up the heat under the frying pan and pour in a further 1 tbsp oil if needed. Add the mushrooms and cook, then transfer the cooked mushrooms into the casserole with the chicken legs. Now fry the onion and carrot with a pinch of salt for 2–3 minutes, until the onion begins to brown at the edges. Add the garlic, thyme, bay leaf and a grinding of black pepper and stir, then transfer the vegetables to the casserole.

Finally, stir the stock into the frying pan, scraping up any sediment with a wooden spoon to dissolve it into the sauce. Pour this over the chicken legs and other ingredients in the casserole, then cover with a lid and set on a medium heat. Simmer for 20 minutes, then add the breasts, replace the lid and cook for 10 more minutes, or until the chicken is cooked.

Strain the liquid into a small pan and simmer over a medium heat – it should taste richly of chicken but not be reduced too much. Taste for seasoning and add salt and pepper if needed. Pour the sauce back over the chicken pieces and reheat. Add the cream, if desired, and simmer for 2–3 minutes.

Serve in deep soup plates with potatoes and a green salad or steamed green beans.

# DUCK LEGS BRAISED WITH SUMMER VEGETABLES

✳ Serves 4 ✳ Preparation time 30 minutes ✳ Cooking time 2 hours

Mrs Beeton's lovely recipe for duck with turnips was made from cold, leftover duck. This version uses raw duck legs, which are a flavourful and inexpensive alternative to using a whole duck. You can substitute other vegetables for the turnips if you prefer.

4 duck legs

1 tbsp sunflower oil

100g streaky bacon, cut into 1cm chunks

1 medium onion, peeled and finely chopped

1 stick celery, finely chopped

1 garlic clove, peeled and sliced

2 bay leaves

1 large thyme sprig

100ml dry white wine

200ml dark chicken stock (see page 67)

200g white turnips, peeled and cut into large chunks

80g peas

salt and freshly ground black pepper

Preheat the oven to 180°C/gas mark 4. Season the duck legs lightly with salt and black pepper. Place the oil in a large non-stick frying pan over a medium heat. Add the duck legs, skin-side down and brown on both sides. Transfer to a baking tray that will fit them snugly.

Pour away most of the fat from the pan and add the bacon, onion and celery. Cook over a low heat, stirring, until the vegetables have picked up a little colour, then add the garlic, bay leaves, thyme and white wine. Turn up the heat and bring to a boil. Reduce the liquid by half, and then stir in the stock. Pour the mixture over the duck legs and top up with enough boiling water to almost cover them.

Cook for 1 hour in the oven then test by inserting a knife into the joint. If the juices run clear, they are cooked. If not, allow another 10–20 minutes. Add the turnips, tucked into the liquid, and return to the oven for a further 20 minutes.

Remove the duck legs from the liquid and place them on a baking sheet. Turn the oven up to 200°C/gas mark 6, and put the legs back into the oven to crisp up for 10–15 minutes.

Meanwhile, skim the fat from the liquid in the baking tray and then strain it into a saucepan (reserving the vegetables) placed over a medium heat. Boil until the liquid has reduced by half. Skim the surface again to remove any fat or scum and then add the peas. Taste the liquid at this stage and correct the seasoning if required. Add the veg and warm through.

To serve, divide the vegetables and liquid among 4 serving bowls and place a duck leg on top of each.

# CURRIED RABBIT

✳ Serves 4 ✳ Preparation time 45 minutes ✳ Cooking time 2 hours 30 minutes–3 hours

Mrs Beeton gives extensive notes on rabbits, including a simple rabbit curry. Here, rather than a generic curry powder as she would have used, a combination of spices is specified, which produces a spicy sauce that balances beautifully with the rich, fruity flavour of a wild rabbit. Serve with aged (high-quality) basmati rice.

6 tbsp sunflower oil

3 onions, finely chopped

1 tsp cumin seeds

2 bay leaves

1 tsp salt

1 tbsp coriander seeds

1 tsp fenugreek seeds

1 tsp ground turmeric

4 garlic cloves, finely chopped

30g piece fresh root ginger, peeled and finely chopped

1 bird's-eye chilli, finely chopped

400g tin chopped tomatoes

1 tbsp tomato purée

1kg rabbit (1 large or 2 small animals), jointed

lemon juice, to taste

2 tbsp chopped coriander, to garnish

to finish

1 garlic clove, peeled

30g piece fresh root ginger, peeled and chopped

50ml double cream

1 tsp garam masala

Place a pan over a high heat and add the oil, chopped onion, cumin seeds, bay leaves and salt. Add enough water to cover the onion and cook until all the water has evaporated. Reduce the heat slightly and fry until golden brown, then add the coriander and fenugreek seeds and the turmeric and fry for 2–3 minutes. Add the chopped garlic, ginger and chilli and fry for another 2–3 minutes then add the tomatoes, tomato purée and rabbit legs. Add 250ml boiling water, cover and cook gently either on the hob or in a low oven at 140°C/gas mark 1 for 2½–3 hours.

Keeping back the legs, pour the sauce into a jug blender with the finishing ingredients and blend for 2–3 minutes. Pass through a sieve back into the pan with the legs, and add the loins. Place in a pan over a low heat. Simmer for 5 minutes, or until the loins are cooked and the legs are heated through. Season everything with salt and fresh lemon juice to adjust the sharpness. Sprinkle with chopped coriander before serving.

**Note:** To cook the rice, soak 100g basmati rice per person in a bowl of cold water for 10 minutes, then rinse and drain. Place a large pan of water on a high heat and when it boils stir in the rice. Bring back to a boil then simmer gently until the rice is almost tender. Add a good pinch of salt. Cook for a few minutes more, until tender. Drain well and return to the pan with the lid on. Leave for 2 minutes, then fluff with a fork.

# VENISON CASSEROLE

✳ Serves 4 ✳ Preparation time 25 minutes ✳ Cooking time 1 hour 30 minutes including resting time

Roe or red deer can usually be bought from a butcher. The allspice berries, which Mrs Beeton recommends, add an agreeable background warmth to this dish. The port she uses in her venison stew gives a sweeter result than wine: use whichever you prefer.

1 tsp allspice berries

1 tsp juniper berries

3 tbsp duck fat or
sunflower oil

800g venison, ideally Roe
or Red shoulder, trimmed of sinew
and cut into 3cm cubes

200g onions, peeled and cut
into large chunks

200g celery, cut into 2cm
pieces

300ml light red wine or port

2 strips rind pared from a
Seville orange or a tangerine

500ml venison, jellied game
or dark chicken stock
(see page 68 or 67)

2 tsp arrowroot, to thicken
(optional)

salt and freshly ground
black pepper

special equipment

a small piece of muslin and a
flameproof casserole

Preheat the oven to 140°C/gas mark 1. Tie the juniper and allspice berries in a piece of muslin and set aside.

Heat 2 tbsp of the fat or oil in a large non-stick frying pan over a high heat. Add the venison cubes and brown them well on all sides, adding a pinch of salt as they brown. Transfer the meat to a flameproof casserole big enough to hold all the pieces in 1–2 layers.

Place a further 1 tbsp fat or oil in the pan over a medium heat. Add the onions and celery with another pinch of salt, and fry. When the onions soften and turn brown at the edges stir everything from the pan into the venison. Add the wine to the frying pan and scrape the caramelised bits from the base of the pan. Add this to the venison along with the rind, stock, and the muslin bag holding the allspice and juniper berries.

Put the lid on the casserole and cook in the oven for 1 hour 15 minutes, or until the venison is tender (this will depend on the age of the animal).

Remove from the oven. The sauce will be like a broth at this point. If you prefer it thicker, add 2 tsp arrowroot to 2 tbsp cold water and stir with a fork, ensuring that the mixture is lump-free. Whisk this into the broth and let it simmer, stirring, for a few minutes. Season to taste if required, and serve with mashed potatoes and buttered cabbage.

# A Note on Venison

The quality of meat of the various deer species, collectively known as venison, depends on the age and gender of the animal. Venison from a male under two years of age will usually be tender. The texture of venison from an older animal will be firmer, but it will taste better. Venison from mature males should be avoided, especially during the rut, because it can have an overly strong flavour.

**Farmed venison**

Red deer are farmed for the flavour and quality of their venison (females are tender and flavoursome up to six years; males up to two years). Wild red deer meat is available, but as it is often produced as part of land management practices, the meat quality is variable. Well-farmed red deer is therefore more likely to offer consistently high quality.

**Wild venison**

Roe deer are never farmed, and if they are shot, most of their meat goes into the catering trade. Fallow deer are larger than roe, and are mostly to be found in deer parks in the UK. They are considered to be a wild managed herd in this instance, and so have a fixed season. Sika and muntjac deer are also common in the UK, but their meat rarely appears on the market.

# FAST
# COOKING

'The wild pigeon, or stockdove, is the parent whence all the varieties of the domestic pigeon are derived. In the wild state it is still found in many parts of this island, making its nest in the holes of rocks, in the hollows of trees, or in old towers, but never like the ringdove, on branches. The blue house-pigeon is the variety principally reared for the table in this country, and is produced from our farmyards in great numbers. When young, and still fed by their parents, they are most preferable for the table. And are called squabs; under six months they are denominated squeakers and at six months they begin to breed. Their flesh is accounted savoury, delicate, and stimulating, and the dark-coloured birds are considered to have the highest flavour, whilst the light are esteemed to have the more delicate flesh.'

*Beeton's Book of Household Management*

# PIGEON & MUSHROOM ON TOAST

❊ Serves 4 ❊ Preparation time 15 minutes ❊ Cooking time 20 minutes including resting time

Mrs Beeton suggested serving mushrooms with pigeon and the two make a winning combination either as a sauce or, as here, simply pan-fried and served on toast to absorb the lovely cooking juices.

85g unsalted butter

8 skinless pigeon breasts

4 small shallots, peeled and finely sliced

2 thyme sprigs

1 bay leaf

200g portobello mushrooms, cut into 1cm chunks

2 garlic cloves, peeled and chopped

50ml white wine

100ml dark chicken stock (see page 67)

small bunch flat-leaf parsley, stems discarded, leaves chopped

lemon juice, to taste

salt and freshly ground black pepper

to serve

4 slices good white bread for toast

salted butter

Preheat the oven to 105°C/gas mark ¼.

Place 50g of the butter in a large frying pan set over a medium to high heat. Season the breasts with ½ tsp salt and then fry in the butter for 1–2 minutes on each side, or until golden brown on the outside and still rare in the centre. Set the breasts on a plate in the oven, covered with foil, to rest while you finish the recipe.

Return the pan to the heat and turn down to medium. Immediately add the shallots, thyme, bay leaf and a few grindings of black pepper. Cook until the shallots are soft and beginning to colour. Add the mushrooms, garlic and another 25g of the butter and cook for 5 minutes.

Add the white wine to the pan and, using a wooden spoon, stir to dislodge any caramelised bits sticking to the bottom of the pan. Stir in the stock then return the breasts to the pan, cook for 5 minutes, and add the remaining butter and parsley. Meanwhile, toast the bread. Adjust the seasoning and stir in a squeeze of lemon juice to freshen up the sauce.

To serve, set a piece of buttered toast on each plate. Place some sauce and mushrooms and 2 breasts on top of each and serve immediately with a simple salad.

# PHEASANT BREASTS WITH CIDER & CREAM

✳ Serves 2 ✳ Preparation time 5 minutes ✳ Cooking time 15 minutes including resting time

This recipe shows how versatile game can be, and that you do not always have to cook a whole bird. Pheasant breasts are widely available now and they cook quickly. This dish is an amalgam of two of Mrs Beeton's recipes, and a modern version of a fricassee (which traditionally was leftover cooked meat with piquant seasoning and cream). If you can't get Hertfordshire cider, any good cider will do.

2 cock pheasant breasts or 3 hen pheasant breasts, weighing 400g in total

1 tbsp sunflower oil

20g cold, unsalted butter

2 shallots, peeled and finely sliced

1 thyme sprig

1 Cox's apple, peeled, cored, and cut into 12 slices

150ml dry Hertfordshire cider

45ml cider brandy or Calvados

150ml double cream

1 tsp green peppercorns, drained

Preheat the oven to 120°C/gas mark ½.

Season each breast with salt and black pepper on the flesh side. Place the oil in a frying pan over a medium to high heat and fry the pheasant skin-side down until it is well browned, then turn over and brown the other side. This should take 2–3 minutes on each side. Remove the breasts to a plate, cover with foil and keep warm.

Place half the butter in the pan over medium heat. Add the shallots and thyme and cook, stirring, for 2 minutes. The shallots will pick up colour from the caramelised juices. When they are lightly browned, add the apple slices. Cook for 30 seconds, turning them once.

Add the cider and return the pheasant breasts to the pan. Cook until all the liquid has evaporated, turning the breasts once or twice to heat through. When the sauce is reduced and sticky, remove it from the heat (and keep it away from any overhanging curtains or blinds), add the Calvados and flame by holding a match to the edge of the pan.

When the flames die down, add the cream and peppercorns. Shake the pan to amalgamate the sauce and simmer for 2–3 minutes. Add the remaining butter to the pan, shake again and serve immediately with buttered noodles and a watercress salad.

# PIGEON & BLOOD ORANGE SALAD

✳ Serves 4 ✳ Preparation time 15 minutes ✳ Cooking time 10 minutes including resting time

Mrs Beeton commonly used citrus fruit with her poultry and game bird recipes. Many of the birds she used are now protected and no longer available for cooking. We can use pigeons, however, which are shot in large numbers in early spring, just when the best citrus fruit is arriving in our shops. Mrs Beeton usually broiled or grilled her birds and served them quite plain, but the breasts can be pan-fried and make a delicious salad.

160g green beans, trimmed

1 blood orange

8 skinless pigeon breasts

30g unsalted butter

1 small shallot, peeled and finely chopped

60g hazelnuts, roasted, peeled and coarsely chopped (see note)

small bunch flat-leaf parsley, stems discarded, leaves finely chopped

small bunch chervil, stems discarded, leaves finely chopped

60g watercress, thick stems removed

salt and freshly ground black pepper

for the dressing

2 tsp sherry vinegar

3 tsp extra virgin olive oil

1 tsp Dijon mustard

Boil the green beans in slightly salted water for 5 minutes until just tender, then drain and plunge into a bowl of iced water. Leave for 2 minutes, drain and set aside.

Using a sharp knife cut the top and bottom off the orange. Cut the skin off, taking the white pith off as well. Cut out each segment and set aside in a small bowl with any spare juice.

Season the pigeon breasts with salt and black pepper. Place a large frying pan over a high heat and add the butter. Add the breasts to the pan and fry for 2 minutes on each side until well browned. Transfer to a plate, cover with foil and leave to rest in a warm place.

Meanwhile, whisk all the dressing ingredients together in a large bowl. Add the beans, orange segments, shallot, nuts and herbs. Toss together, and then add the watercress, mixing the leaves in thoroughly.

Cut the pigeon breasts in half horizontally and place 4 halves on each plate. Serve the salad alongside the breasts and drizzle over any dressing left in the bowl.

**Note:** To roast hazelnuts, preheat the oven to 180°C/gas mark 4 and place the nuts in a single layer on a baking sheet. Bake for 10–15 minutes, watching them closely, as they will burn quickly. While the nuts are warm, loosen the skins by rubbing the nuts between two tea towels. Discard the skins, spread the nuts out on a cutting board to cool completely then chop them to the desired texture.

# PAN-FRIED HARE LOIN

✱ Serves 2 ✱ Preparation time 10 minutes ✱ Cooking time 20 minutes including resting time

Hare has splendid, rich, dark meat and a large specimen will easily feed six people. Here, the loin is cooked with bacon, lemon and parsley, which are among Mrs Beeton's favourite flavourings for game. It is a quick but special dish that deserves a good bottle of red wine and equally good company.

2 boned hare loin fillets, one from each side of the hare's back

40g unsalted butter

50g streaky bacon, cut into small dice

1 shallot, peeled and finely sliced

1 small bay leaf

small sprig rosemary

½ garlic clove, peeled

30ml red wine

salt and freshly ground black pepper

lemon juice, to taste

small bunch parsley, stems discarded, leaves chopped

special equipment

a temperature probe

Trim the hare loins of all their silver skin and sinew. This is most easily done by laying the strips of meat on your board, silver skin side down. Using a very sharp knife, cut into one end of the meat between the muscle and the silver skin, then cut horizontally across the underside of the meat, keeping your knife close to the board, effectively skinning it as you would a fillet of fish. Then cut them in half to make 4 shorter pieces in total – 2 thick and 2 slightly thinner, tapering pieces. Season the meat with a little salt.

Place a frying pan over a medium to high heat and add half of the butter. When it sizzles, add the 2 thick pieces of loin. Fry for 2 minutes on each side, then add the 2 thinner pieces. Continue to cook for 2–3 minutes, until everything is nicely browned but very pink inside. When a temperature probe inserted in the thickest piece of meat reads 50°C remove the meat from the pan and leave it to rest in a warm place, covered with foil to stop it drying out.

Add the bacon to the pan and fry until golden, then add the shallot, bay leaf, rosemary, garlic and a few grindings of black pepper. Cook for a few minutes until the vegetables are beginning to colour then add the wine. Reduce the liquid by half then stir in the remaining butter. Return the meat to the pan to warm for 1 minute.

Slice the meat thinly and divide between 2 dinner plates. Season the sauce and add a squeeze of lemon to taste. Stir in the chopped parsley and spoon the sauce over the meat. Serve with steamed kale or braised turnips.

# PAN-FRIED VENISON LOIN
## WITH WHITE WINE, CREAM & MUSTARD

✱ Serves 4 ✱ Preparation time 10 minutes ✱ Cooking time 15 minutes including resting time

The loin of any animal (that section between the top of the pelvis and the ribcage) is a prime cut. Though tender, in the case of venison it is best cooked medium to keep it juicy. Mrs Beeton tended to cook meat either as whole joints or gave recipes for leftovers cooked as fricassees, probably because this suited the ovens, fires and spits of her day. Today we are used to cooking meat on the top of the stove, a style this recipe illustrates perfectly.

4 x 160–200g pieces of red or roe venison loin

1 tbsp sunflower oil

½ tsp salt

1 tsp cracked black pepper

1 tsp crushed juniper berries

20g unsalted butter, plus an extra knob

2 shallots, peeled and finely chopped

1 bay leaf

75ml dry white wine

100ml dark chicken or jellied game stock (see page 67 or 68)

150ml single cream

2 tsp Dijon mustard

Preheat the oven to 120°C/gas mark ½ and place a large plate in the oven. Trim the venison pieces or loin of all skin and fat and cut into pieces about 12–15cm long. Place the pieces in a shallow bowl, add the sunflower oil and ½ tsp salt and toss to coat.

Place a large frying pan over high heat. Add the loins and sear on all sides for about 7–8 minutes, or until they are evenly dark brown all over. Start with a high heat and turn the heat down once the meat has begun to brown. Add the pepper and juniper berries and cook for 1–2 minutes, then transfer the loins to the warm plate in the oven and cover with foil. Leave for 5 minutes while you finish the sauce.

Drain any oil from the pan and set it over a medium heat. To the spices remaining in the pan add the butter, shallots and a small pinch of salt. Fry until the shallots brown at the edges, then add the bay leaf, white wine and stock.

Turn the heat to high and bring to a boil. Allow the liquid to reduce to a sticky glaze, then turn the heat down to low, add the cream and simmer, scraping all the sediment and juices from the bottom of the pan into the sauce. Stir in the Dijon mustard and a knob of unsalted butter, and then return the loins to the pan along with any juices from the plate. Once everything has warmed through, slice the loins on the diagonal into long slices and serve with the sauce.

PIES &
TERRINES

# A Note on Pies

The pie has a fond place in the heart of the English kitchen. Pastry, meat and gravy, well seasoned and well baked, to eat either hot or cold takes a central place in many weekday meals. Visit any Scottish baker and you will see schoolchildren lined up at lunch for their scotch pies, made in unwieldy variety. Over the centuries, since early pastries were codified and written in the late 16th century, the ingredients used to make them, and the different ways pastry is made, evolved hugely.

By the time Isabella compiled the recipes for the first edition of *Beeton's Book of Household Management*, many modern pastry recipes were established. True to form, Isabella, along with other Victorian writers, listed absolute measurements, knowing that her contemporaries might not have been in a position to learn, by hand, from their forebears. Various recipes for pastes – read pastry – appear in the book including several she borrowed from named chefs such as Soyer and Ude, considered to be two of the finest chefs working in England at the time.

The game terrine on page 57 uses a fine paste made with butter and eggs, designed to be eaten with its contents, as opposed to early pastes which were often just used to contain and preserve fillings. The butter and eggs it contains help it to withstand the moisture in the pie, but the jelly really holds the whole together, glueing the pastry and filling – but also making the pie a complete whole, transmitting the savoury flavour of the filling and seasoning to your tastebuds as it melts sublimely.

# CHICKEN PIE

✳ Serves 6 ✳ Preparation time 2 hours 30 minutes ✳ Cooking time 45 minutes

Mrs Beeton used a mixture of chicken with ham, eggs and forcemeat in her fowl pie, in a complicated mixture that would mask the delicate flavours of a modern chicken. In this simplified recipe, the carcass is browned to flavour the stock, making use of every part of the bird. The meat, sauce and pastry can all be made a day ahead, if you like.

1 quantity flaky shortcrust pastry (see page 56)

2kg whole chicken, jointed, carcass reserved

1 tbsp sunflower oil

1 onion, peeled and roughly chopped

1 carrot, peeled and roughly chopped

1 bay leaf

1 thyme sprig

150g ham, cut into small chunks

15g unsalted butter

150g mushrooms, chopped roughly if large

2 medium leeks, trimmed and cut into 1cm slices

200ml double cream, plus extra to glaze the pie

plain flour, for dusting

salt and freshly ground black pepper

special equipment

a roasting tin, a deep 22–25cm pie dish and a temperature probe

Make the shortcrust pastry and keep it covered and chilled until ready to use. Preheat the oven to 200°C/gas mark 6. Toss the chicken joints and carcass in the sunflower oil in a large roasting tin to coat and season with a little salt. Roast for 30 minutes, then remove the breasts. Continue to cook legs, wings and carcass for 15 minutes, or until well browned, then remove from the oven.

Chill the breast pieces while you make the stock. Place the onion, carrot, bay leaf, thyme and chicken legs, wings and carcass into a large saucepan. Add 800ml cold water and place over a medium heat. Bring to a simmer and cook for 30 minutes.

Once cooked, strain the chicken stock and spoon off any fat from the surface. Pull the meat from the bones and place it in a large bowl, adding the breast meat pulled into chunks. Add the ham.

Heat the butter in a frying pan over a medium heat. Add the mushrooms and fry until lightly browned. Add the leeks and enough stock to cover. Simmer for 2–3 minutes until the leeks are tender. Add the mushrooms and leeks to the chicken, leaving the liquid in the pan. Pour in the remaining stock and cream. Season to taste with salt and black pepper, then pour over the chicken and mix thoroughly. Cool the pie filling while you prepare the pastry, or chill and finish the pie the following day.

Preheat the oven to 200°C/gas mark 6. Place the filling in the pie dish, piling it up in the middle. Flour your work surface and roll the pastry into a neat circle 10cm larger than your pie dish and around 4–5mm thick. Any offcuts can be used to decorate the lid of the pie.

Moisten the edge of the dish with water. Trim 4mm from around the edge of the pastry, moisten it and attach it to the rim of the pie dish. Moisten the top of the strip with a little water, then take the circle of pastry and drape it over the pie dish, pinching around the edge to make a seal. Trim the edges of any surplus pastry and reserve for decorating the pie. Cut a small hole in the top of the pie to let the steam escape and decorate the lid with pastry leaves made from the surplus pastry, sticking these down with water.

Brush the pie with a little cream and bake for 45 minutes, or until the pastry is well browned and crisp. When a temperature probe placed in the centre of the pie reads 80°C the pie is ready. If not, turn the heat down to 150°C/gas mark 2 and continue cooking until the insides come up to temperature. If the pastry begins to burn, cover it with foil.

**Note:** A large rabbit can be treated in the same fashion – simply joint the animal and braise all of the parts as the above recipe does for the chicken legs, ensuring it is tender before making the sauce. If you like, you can slice the liver and add it to the mushrooms to cook briefly before adding the leeks.

# FLAKY SHORTCRUST PASTRY

✱ Makes enough for 1 x 22–25cm pie  ✱ Preparation time 10 minutes plus 1 hour chilling time

Mrs Beeton gives a recipe for a 'medium puff paste' that is a halfway house between shortcrust and puff pastry, but made in the same way as puff pastry. The recipe here achieves the same result with far less fuss. A portion of the fat is blended with the flour mixture while the remainder is added in small lumps. These melt as it bakes, giving the resulting pastry a delicious, yielding flakiness. This pastry is excellent for using in pies.

250g plain flour

pinch salt

150g cold unsalted butter

½ tsp lemon juice

100ml iced water

If you have a food processor, sift the flour and salt into the bowl and mix. Cut 100g of the butter into rough cubes and add them to the flour mixture. Pulse until it resembles fine breadcrumbs. Cut the rest of the butter into small cubes, add them the blender and pulse briefly to combine. Small lumps of butter should still be obvious in the mixture.

If you are working by hand, sift the flour and salt into a large bowl. Coarsely grate 100g of the butter into the flour mixture. Rub the butter and flour between your fingertips working quickly to keep the mixture as cool as possible. If it starts to feel sticky, chill the mixture for 30 minutes. Then coarsely grate the remaining butter into the mixture and stir. Small lumps or strands of butter should be clearly visible.

Chill the mixture for 30 minutes. Just before you are ready to proceed, stir the lemon juice into the water and pour two-thirds of this into the flour mixture. Blend well with a fork, stirring quickly but gently. Using your fingertips, bring the dough together, adding more water as necessary (you may need to use all of it) until everything is evenly mixed and there are no dry lumps of flour. Bring the mixture together into a smooth, supple lump, carefully form it into a flattened ball, wrap in cling film and chill for at least 1 hour before use.

# GAME TERRINE

✳ Serves 8 ✳ Preparation time 1 hour ✳ Cooking time 1 hour 40 minutes plus 2–3 days chilling time

This recipe makes a lovely lunch or supper dish from just one bird, either a wild duck or small (hen) pheasant, or the equivalent weight of any game meat. Mrs Beeton used forcemeat in her recipe; here, minced pork and seasoning are used instead, as they are more easily available today. Just ask your butcher to coarsely mince some fatty pork, which will baste the meat as it cooks. This is best made a few days before you plan to serve it.

for the pastry

300g plain flour

large pinch salt

200g cold salted butter, cubed

1 medium egg

1 tsp lemon juice

for the filling

1 large wild duck (to yield 225g breast meat

and 120g leg meat)

750g coarsely minced fatty pork, such as belly

1 medium egg, beaten

for the seasoning

1 garlic clove, crushed

2 tsp salt

1 tsp ground mace

½ tsp black pepper

1 tbsp chopped fresh thyme

for the jelly

2 leaves gelatine

200ml jellied game stock (page 68)

50ml Marsala

special equipment

a 1kg terrine dish or loaf tin

To make the pastry, sift the flour and salt into the bowl of your food processor and add the cubed butter. Pulse until the mixture resembles fine breadcrumbs then transfer it to a large bowl. If you are working by hand, sift the flour and salt into a bowl. Cut the butter into very small cubes, or grate it finely. Add it to the bowl and, working quickly, rub the butter into the flour using your fingertips. If it starts to feel sticky, chill the mixture for 30 minutes before continuing.

Combine the egg, lemon juice and 4 tablespoons of cold water and stir two-thirds of this mixture into the flour and butter using a large fork. Now bring the mixture together with your fingertips into a supple, but not sticky, dough, adding more liquid as necessary. Gently form the dough into a ball, cover with cling film and chill for at least 30 minutes

Meanwhile, line a 1kg terrine dish or loaf tin with a strip of non-stick baking paper, leaving a 2cm overhang along the long sides of the tin to help you lift the terrine from the tin for serving.

Remove the breasts from the duck, discard the skin and slice into strips. Set aside.

Remove the meat and skin from the legs, scraping the flesh from the bones with a small knife. Pull out any hard white tendons from the drumstick meat as you cut. Put the leg meat into the bowl of a food processor and pulse to reduce it to a fine paste. Add the minced pork.

Combine the seasoning ingredients together in a bowl and sprinkle 2 pinches of the mixture over the breasts. Mix the rest of the seasoning in with the leg meat mixture.

Preheat the oven to 200°C/gas mark 6.

Roll out 300g of the pastry and use it to line the base and sides of the loaf tin in one piece, allowing it to overhang the sides a little so that you can create a good seal when the lid is on.

Fill the pastry case with alternating layers of leg meat mixture and breast meat, ending with a layer of leg meat mixture.

Roll out the remaining pastry to make a lid. Place it on top of the pie and seal it by tightly crimping the pastry edges, folding the bottom layer over the top and pinching the two together with your fingertips. Shape any trimmings into leaves to decorate the top, sealing them in place with a little water, then brush the lid with the beaten egg. Finally, cut a small hole in the top of the pie and insert a rolled-up piece of greaseproof paper to act as a funnel.

Bake the pie for 25 minutes then turn the oven down to 180°C/gas mark 4. After 45 minutes turn the oven down to 160°C/gas mark 3 and bake for a final 30 minutes, then cool in the tin.

When the pie is almost cold, prepare the jelly. Soak the gelatine sheets in a small bowl of cold water for 10 minutes. Meanwhile place a small pan over low heat.

Add the stock and Marsala and let it warm until it is hand-hot. Squeeze the water from the gelatine leaves and add them to the warm stock, stirring to dissolve. Very slowly and carefully pour the jelly through the hole in the top of the pie, allowing it time to filter into the terrine. Chill, in the tin, ideally for 2–3 days before serving. When you are ready to serve, dip the terrine tin into a bowl of hot water for 1–2 minutes. Holding on to the overhanging baking paper, lift the pie from the tin, peel away the paper and place on a serving dish. The terrine is delicious served sliced with apple chutney and a salad of chicory leaves dressed with a little oil and either raspberry or sherry vinegar, or simply with pickles.

STOCKS,
SOUPS &
GRAVY

# A Note on Stocks

These words are as true today as when Mrs Beeton wrote them: good stocks are the essence of good cooking. Stocks are the foundation of so many dishes, so it is worth ensuring that they contain only the best ingredients. Take care never to over-season stock. Many recipes call for stocks to be reduced, so a stock that starts off already slightly salty will result in a very salty finished dish.

Unlike in Mrs Beeton's time, ready-made stocks in liquid or powdered form are now widely available. However, they are rarely based on prime ingredients or made with the care you would take when making your own. Ready-made stock almost never has the body of homemade stock – a quality that derives from using gelatinous meat and bones to make the homemade version – so will give a completely different result to the recipes it is used in. Many ready-made stocks are also salty, and so not suitable for reducing.

For all these reasons, it really is worth saving up some bones, setting aside some time, and making your own. Because stock takes some time to cook, it may help to roast any bones and vegetables the day before and chill them overnight before proceeding when you have a full day available.

Adding cold water and a few vegetables and seasoning to raw, roasted or browned meat and bones makes meat stock. Slowly heating the mixture brings fat and scum to the surface. Skimming the impurities and fat away with a large metal spoon or ladle as the stock cooks produces clear, brilliant stock. On no account should stock be allowed to boil until it has been skimmed, strained, and all fat removed. Then, the stock may safely be boiled to reduce it, skimming again to remove any impurities that may rise to the surface.

When stock is finished and cold, any traces of fat that remain on the surface can be removed and discarded and the stock frozen for use later. Freezing stock in re-sealable containers that hold 250ml or 500ml portions will prove useful for most recipes. Alternatively, or to use up any extra, you can freeze stock in ice-cube trays for adding flavour to sauces.

Mrs Beeton's original book listed three main meat stocks, each containing a mixture of meats. However, it is accepted today that a good stock should give an unmistakeable, unadulterated essence of a single type of meat that will complement, not interfere with, the flavour of the finished dish. For this reason, the stocks given in this chapter are modern ones, not taken from or influenced by Mrs Beeton but intended to complement and update her other recipes.

## Ingredients

✳ Bones should be fresh and trimmed of any excess fat. Those that have a good proportion of cartilage, such as knuckles, feet and ribs, are excellent for stock as the gelatine they contain gives the stock body.

✳ Vegetables should be good quality and fresh. Wash them well and peel them if necessary before chopping or trimming them. Unless the recipe specifies otherwise, always use medium -sized vegetables.

✳ Herbs should be tied together in small bundles (called faggots in Mrs Beeton's day) using kitchen string so they are easy to retrieve from the stock once it has finished cooking.

✳ Cold water, rather than hot, should be added to stocks as it encourages fat to rise and solidify, making it easier to skim from the surface.

✳ Wine, if you use it, should be or drinking quality and not dregs or anything past its best.

✳ Salt should only be added at the end. As you reduce the stock it will intensify the natural salts within the ingredients, so you should never add salt until the stock is fully reduced and you have tasted it. You can always add more seasoning at a later stage, if desired, but you can't repair over-salted stock.

## Making gravy

Gravy is the sauce made from the caramelised juices of roasted meat left behind in the roasting tin. Adding wine and/or stock to this makes the gravy base, but if you are using wine, allow it to boil for a minute to burn off the alcohol first. Then thicken the liquid with beurre manié, or cornflour or arrowroot mixed with a little water, as described above. Simmer, stirring, to loosen any caramelised bits still adhering to the roasting tin, and to allow the thickener to finish cooking. When the gravy has cooked, allow it to sit for a minute then spoon off any fat that floats to the surface, or use a separating jug.

# CLARIFYING STOCKS

✳ To clarify 2 litres of stock  ✳ Preparation time 10 minutes  ✳ Cooking time 20–30 minutes

Clarification is a method used to clear stocks that have clouded or need to be refined for use in a consommé. Mrs Beeton noted that, 'when [a stock] is obliged to be clarified it is deteriorated both in quality and flavour', yet she did include a recipe for clarifying stocks, which calls for a simple mixture of egg whites and water, in her book. This updated recipe uses a similar method, but retains the flavour by using a mixture of minced, lean meat of the same type as the stock being clarified, plus vegetables, herbs and spices. You need to start with cold stock so that the egg white solidifies gradually, trapping particles from the stock as it does so.

2 litres cold chicken or jellied game stock (see pages 66–67 or 68)

120g egg white (about 3 large or 4 medium egg whites)

30g carrot, peeled and roughly chopped

50g onion, peeled and roughly chopped

20g celery, trimmed and roughly chopped

20g leek, trimmed and roughly chopped

200g lean, minced chicken or beef

few thyme sprigs

1 bay leaf

1 garlic clove, peeled

1 tsp black peppercorns

Place the cold stock into a large saucepan. Put the egg white, vegetables and meat in the jug of a food processor and pulse to chop to a coarse paste.

Turn the heat under the saucepan to high and whisk the vegetable and egg paste, the herbs, garlic and peppercorns into the stock. Bring to a gentle simmer over a high heat, whisking again once or twice as it warms. At no point should the stock be allowed to bubble.

As the stock reaches a simmer, the egg and vegetables begin to form a thick scum on the surface. Reduce the heat to low and keep the stock just under a simmer. The surface layer will thicken and set, trapping all of the sediment and debris.

After 10 minutes, remove the pan from heat and break a hole in the egg crust large enough to fit the bowl of a ladle through. Very carefully ladle the stock out through the hole and into a muslin-lined sieve suspended over a large bowl.

Cover and chill immediately and use as required. This will yield approximately 1.8 litres, and can be stored in the freezer for up to 2 months.

# LIGHT CHICKEN STOCK

✳ Makes 1.5 litres  ✳ Preparation time 10 minutes  ✳ Cooking time 3 hours

Light chicken stock is used in delicately flavoured dishes, which would be masked by a more intensely flavoured stock. It is also useful for lighter soups, or for braising young vegetables such as turnips or beetroot.

**1.5kg chicken wings and thighs, raw**

**1 large carrot, roughly chopped**

**2 onions, roughly chopped**

**2 sticks celery, roughly chopped**

**2 bay leaves**

**small bunch thyme**

special equipment

**a large stockpot**

Place all the ingredients into the stockpot over a medium heat. Cover with cold water to a depth of 5–10cm and bring to a gentle simmer. Continue to simmer for 2 hours, making sure the stock does not boil at any point and skimming as necessary. Strain the stock through a fine sieve or chinois into a large bowl. Leave it to cool, then cover and chill.

Carefully remove any fat from the top of the chilled stock and pour it back into the cleaned stockpot. Bring to a boil over a high heat to reduce the stock until you are left with 1.5 litres. Remove from the heat and cool, then pour into re-sealable 250ml containers and freeze for up to 2 months.

# DARK CHICKEN STOCK

✱ Makes 1.5 litres  ✱ Preparation time 1 hour 15 minutes  ✱ Cooking time 6 hours

This full-flavoured chicken stock is made from browned, roasted chicken bones and pieces. It has an intense flavour and light gelatinous body and is excellent with strongly flavoured poultry and game dishes that can stand up to a robust stock.

**1.5kg chicken wings and thighs**

**2 tbsp sunflower oil**

**1 large carrot, roughly chopped**

**2 onions, roughly chopped**

**2 sticks celery, roughly chopped**

**2 bay leaves**

**small bunch thyme**

special equipment

**a roasting tin and a large stockpot**

Preheat the oven to 220°C/gas mark 7. Arrange the chicken wings and thighs in a roasting tin and set in the oven. Cook, turning occasionally, for 1 hour, or until the pieces are deep golden-brown in colour.

When the chicken is nearly cooked, place the oil in a large stockpot over medium heat. Add vegetables and fry until lightly coloured. Add the cooked chicken to the pan. Pour off and discard any excess fat in the roasting tin.

Pour a little water into the roasting tin and stir, scraping up any caramelised juices. Pour these into the pan with the vegetables and chicken.

Finally, add the herbs to the chicken and vegetables and pour enough cold water into the stockpot to cover the chicken and vegetables to a depth of 10cm. Turn the heat to high and bring the stock to a simmer, then reduce the heat. Make sure the stock does not boil at any point and skim off any scum that rises to the surface while it is simmering.

After 5 hours, strain the stock through a fine sieve or chinois into a large bowl. Leave it to cool, then cover and chill.

Once it is completely cold, carefully remove any fat from the top. Pour the stock back into the cleaned stockpot, place over a high heat and bring to a boil. Reduce the stock until you are left with 1.5 litres. Remove from the heat to cool, then chill until cold, pour into re-sealable 250ml containers and freeze for up to 2 months. To use, allow the stock to thaw out.

# JELLIED GAME STOCK

✳ Makes 2 litres ✳ Preparation time 1 hour 45 minutes ✳ Cooking time 8 hours

The backbones of game birds can be bitter, so do not use them in stocks. When using giblets, always check them for green or yellow stains. These indicate contamination with bile, and any affected parts should be cut off and discarded.

750g pheasant carcass
(backbone discarded) or
other game bones and meat

750g pork rib bones

2 tbsp sunflower oil

2 large onions, roughly
chopped

1 carrot, roughly chopped

1 stick celery, roughly chopped

1 garlic clove, peeled
and sliced in half

2 bay leaves

1 thyme sprig

500ml white wine

special equipment

1–2 roasting tins and
a large stockpot

Preheat the oven to 200°C/gas mark 6. Place the bones in a large roasting tin, drizzle with the oil and toss to coat. If you cannot fit the pieces in a single layer use 2 tins. Place in the oven and roast, turning every 20 minutes, until well browned. After 1 hour add the chopped vegetables, garlic and herbs, turning everything occasionally so nothing burns.

After 30 minutes remove from the oven, pour off and discard any fat, and then place the contents of the roasting tin into a stockpot.

Add the wine to the roasting tin or tins and use a wooden spoon to scrape any sediment from the bottom, warming the tins over a low heat to dissolve the juices if necessary, then pour everything from the roasting tins into the stockpot.

Add enough cold water to cover the bones to a depth of 10cm. Bring the stock to a simmer and skim off any fat or scum that rises to the surface. Then turn the heat down to low and leave the stock to simmer very slowly for 6 hours. When cooked, strain the stock through a very fine sieve or chinois into a large bowl, cover and chill.

Once cold, skim any fat from the surface. Pour the stock back into the cleaned stockpot and bring to a boil over a high heat. Reduce to approximately 2 litres, skimming as necessary. Remove the stockpot from the heat and leave to cool. Then chill until cold, pour into re-sealable 250ml containers and freeze for up to 2 months.

Allow the stock to thaw out, then dilute with an equal quantity of water, before using in game soups, braises and casseroles.

# WILD DUCK & MUSHROOM BROTH

✳ Serves ✳ Preparation time 15 minutes ✳ Cooking time 1 hour 15 minutes

This recipe is inspired by Mrs Beeton's regency soup, which is designed to use up 'any bones and remains of any cold game, such as of pheasants, partridges, etc'. Mushrooms, used here, particularly suit the flavour of wild duck. One leftover roast domestic duck leg would be roughly equivalent to the 4 wild duck legs listed in the ingredients. If you use raw duck legs, remove the skin and increase the initial cooking time for the legs to 1 hour.

4 wild duck legs leftover from roast ducks or raw

1 bay leaf

1 litre dark chicken stock or jellied game stock (see page 67 or 68)

2 tbsp light olive oil

2 large onions, peeled and finely chopped

100g (peeled weight) celeriac, finely chopped

80g carrot, peeled and chopped

10g butter

250g portobello mushrooms, sliced thickly

½ tsp thyme leaves

pinch ground allspice

salt and freshly ground black pepper

Place the duck legs, bay leaf and stock into a saucepan, bring to a simmer and then reduce the heat and put the lid on the pan. Cook for 45 minutes then remove from the heat.

Lift out the legs, leaving the liquid behind in the pan. When the legs are cool enough to handle, remove and discard the skin. Shred the meat and return it to the pan with the liquid.

Meanwhile, prepare the soup base. Place the oil in a saucepan over a medium heat. Add the onion and cook for 2–3 minutes, until it begins to sizzle a little. Add the celeriac, carrot and a pinch of salt. Reduce the heat and cook, stirring occasionally, for 10 minutes.

Set a frying pan over a medium heat and add the butter, the mushrooms and a pinch of salt. Cook, stirring, until the mushrooms begin to brown. Add them to the vegetables in the pan and then add the stock and duck meat, thyme and allspice.

Bring the broth to a simmer over a medium heat, season to taste and serve.

# PHEASANT & CHESTNUT SOUP

✱ Serves 4  ✱ Preparation time 15 minutes  ✱ Cooking time 1 hour

Sweet and aromatic, this soup uses the leftover legs from roast or pot-roast pheasants, but you can use raw legs if you don't have any roasted. The chestnuts add a depth and richness to the light, gamey meat. Mrs Beeton had a pheasant soup and a chestnut one, but the idea of combining the two is new.

1 litre stock left over from pot-roast pheasant (see note) or light chicken stock (see page 66)

legs and thighs of 2 pheasants

1 tbsp light olive oil

1 large onion, peeled and finely chopped

1 stick celery, trimmed and finely chopped

½ carrot, peeled and finely chopped

1 bay leaf

100g peeled cooked chestnuts, chopped

½ tsp chopped thyme

1 tbsp chopped parsley

1 tbsp lemon zest

salt and freshly ground black pepper

Place the stock in a saucepan over a medium heat. Add the pheasant legs and simmer for 40 minutes, or until tender. Remove the meat from the stock and when cool enough to handle, strip all the meat from the bones and shred into pieces no longer than 3cm.

Measure the liquid left in the saucepan. You will need 750ml in total, so add a little water or stock if you are short.

Place the oil in a clean saucepan over a medium heat. Add the vegetables, bay leaf and a pinch of salt and fry until soft but not browned. Add the stock and simmer for 15 minutes.

When the vegetables are tender add the meat, chestnuts and thyme. Continue to simmer for 2–3 minutes then check the seasoning. Garnish with the chopped parsley and lemon zest and serve.

**Note:** To make a stock from the leftovers of the pot-roast pheasant on page 24, reserve the legs and carcass. Using poultry shears, cut out and discard the backbone, then simmer the legs and carcass for 40 minutes with any remaining stock made up to a volume of 1 litre with water.

ON THE
TABLE

# A Note on Preserves

Preserving food that would otherwise be wasted, by making jams and pickles, is an old technique that is still valued in the British kitchen. Fruit can be preserved in many ways, using sugar, salt, vinegar and heat, often in combination, to inhibit the growth of microbes that cause food to spoil.

## Equipment

**Pans**: For the best results, a large, heavy, stainless steel maslin pan is essential. Most of the pans on the market are of 9-litre capacity, with graded metric and imperial measurements on the inside. Buy one with two handles for ease of pouring. Aluminium pans are not suitable for making most preserves because the metal is easily dissolved by the fruit acids and vinegars you will be using.

**Jam funnels:** A wide-necked jam funnel is very useful when transferring hot preserves into jars. These can be metal or silicone. Before using, sterilise them in boiling water for two or three minutes.

**Jars:** Any modern glass jars should be suitable for preserves, but they will need to withstand temperatures of up to 120°C, because they must be sterilised in a low oven before use. Jar lids with rubberised seals must be boiled for 2–3 minutes to sterilise them. Kilner jars with rubber seals and clasps are excellent for this purpose.

Whatever you use, it is important to get a good seal to prevent drying out or spoilage. Metal lids are not appropriate for most preserves because fruit acids and vinegars will dissolve the metal. Plastic lids can be used, as can waxed-paper discs and cellophane, secured well with string or elastic band.

## The cold-saucer test

Mixtures of fruit and sugar will come to a boil at a temperature over 100°C. As the water is driven off by boiling, the temperature will increase and the sugar concentration will rise. To test for temperature, make sure that your thermometer or probe is held in the main body of the jam. If it is held too near the bottom or top the reading will be inaccurate. As the mixture approaches 105°C, it will noticeably thicken, because at this point the pectin will begin to gel together to form a mesh. How long this takes depends on many factors, such as sugar content and acidity.

Before beginning your jelly, put one or two saucers in the fridge to cool. To test how far the pectin has meshed (in other words, if the jam or jelly has reached a setting point), spoon a small amount of the mixture onto one of the cold saucers. Let it sit for a minute, then push the edge with your finger. The surface should wrinkle. If it does not, cook the jam for a couple more minutes, then test again.

# APPLE JELLY

✳ Makes approx 2.4kg – 5 or 6 jars  ✳ Preparation time 20 minutes
✳ Cooking time 1 hour 30 minutes spread over 2 days

A handy jelly to have in the larder, this is lovely on toast and great with game. Bramleys
work well here, but if you use a different variety of cooking apple, adjust the sugar to taste.

**2½kg Bramley apples,
freshly picked or slightly
under-ripe**

**approx 1.6kg jam sugar**

**juice of 3 lemons**

special equipment

**a sugar thermometer or
temperature probe**

Peel the apples and chop into small pieces. Place in a stainless
steel pan and add enough cold water to just cover – about
2 litres. Bring to the boil over a high heat, then simmer gently,
topping up as necessary to ensure the apples remain just
covered, until the fruit is completely broken down and soft.
Strain the hot cooked apples through a jelly bag or a muslin-
lined sieve over a large bowl, and leave to drip overnight if
possible. From these quantities, you should expect a yield of
about 1.8kg pulp (this can be used in place of the quince pulp
in the recipe for quince cheese – see page 79) and 2 litres juice.

When you are ready to finish the jelly, place your clean jars
on a baking sheet in a cool oven at 120°C/gas mark ½, and
place a couple of saucers in the fridge for testing the set of the
jelly when finished. Measure the juice. For every 500ml juice,
weigh out 400g jam sugar. Place the juice and sugar in a large
pan over a high heat, stirring continuously until the sugar has
dissolved. Add the lemon juice, mix well and then divide the
mixture into two roughly equal parts (this will enable to you
to finish the jelly quickly, preserving the flavour).

Bring one half to a rapid rolling boil and cook until it reaches
105°C, stirring frequently to prevent sticking. Begin to test for
setting point when it starts to thicken, using the cold-saucer
method on page 74. Once a setting point has been reached,
remove the jelly from the heat and allow it to form a skin.

Remove and discard any scum that has formed and pot the
jelly into the sterilised jars. Cover the surface of the jelly with
a waxed-paper disc and seal the jar with cellophane. Repeat
the process with the other half of the mixture.

# APPLE SAUCE

✳ Serves 4 ✳ Preparation time 10 minutes ✳ Cooking time 15 minutes

Mrs Beeton would have used an old variety of apple for her sauce. Our now ubiquitous Bramley had only just been discovered and the first trees did not appear for sale until after her book was published. The butter adds natural sweetness, while the new additions of bay leaf and shallot lend a savoury note that makes this sauce more appealing to the modern palate. Serve with cooked game, pork or poultry.

20g unsalted butter

1 shallot, peeled and finely chopped

1 bay leaf

2 large cooking apples, peeled, cored and chopped into small pieces

pinch salt

sugar, to taste

Place the butter in a small saucepan over a medium heat. Add the shallot and bay leaf. Cook for 2–3 minutes, stirring. Add the finely chopped apple and cook until the apple begins to break down. Add a splash of water as the apple cooks to keep it just moist enough to prevent it catching or burning. Add the salt and a little sugar to taste. Continue to cook, stirring occasionally, until the apple is soft. Cool, remove the bay leaf and serve at room temperature.

# APPLE CHUTNEY

✳ Makes approx 3.7kg – 8 to 10 jars ✳ Preparation time 25 minutes ✳ Cooking time 1 hour

Chutneys, along with many other spiced ketchups and sauces, were often brought home to the British kitchen by military gentlemen who had developed a taste for the exotic while overseas. We are now able to buy fresh spices imported monthly into Europe. This must be taken into consideration when looking at the quantities used in historic kitchens, where spices would have invariably taken many months to arrive from abroad, resulting in considerable loss of flavour. This chutney offers a superb way to use up a glut of apples. Its warm, autumnal spice mix, based largely on coriander seeds, works exceptionally well with apple.

**2kg Bramley or other cooking apples, peeled and cored weight**

**1kg shallots, peeled and finely sliced**

**500g sultanas**

**300g soft brown sugar**

**300g granulated sugar**

**1 litre cider vinegar**

**2 tbsp whole coriander seeds**

**1 tsp ground ginger**

**1 tsp ground cinnamon**

special equipment

**a stainless steel preserving pan**

Place the washed jars on a baking sheet in a cool oven, 120°C/ gas mark ½.

Chop the apples into 1cm dice and add to a large stainless steel pan with all the other ingredients. Place the pan on a high heat and bring to a boil, stirring to dissolve the sugar. Simmer on a medium-high heat, stirring regularly, until the chutney is thick. This will take approximately 1 hour depending on the size of the pan and the surface area from which the liquid is evaporating. Take great care not to let the chutney burn – you will have to stir constantly as it begins to thicken, scraping the bottom of the pan carefully with a heatproof spatula or wooden spoon.

When the chutney is ready, place it into the sterilised jars. Seal and store in a cool, dark place for at least 1 month and then use within a year of making.

# QUINCE CHEESE

✳ Makes 2.1kg – 4 or 5 jars  ✳ Preparation time 30 minutes  ✳ Cooking time 4 hours

Quince trees, with their delicate pink flowers, have long been popular in British gardens, but in the last 150 years their fruit has declined in popularity. However, thanks to renewed interest in traditional English produce, it is once again becoming more widely available.

**1½kg pear or Japonica quinces**

**approx 2kg granulated sugar**

If you are using pear quinces, rub off any fur. Wash and chop the fruit into small pieces, including the peel and cores. Discard any black or brown pieces.

Place the quinces in a large stainless steel pan. Cover with water and bring to the boil over a high heat, then turn down to the lowest setting and cook until all the quince pieces are tender. Do not cover, but stir occasionally to prevent sticking and to ensure that the fruit is evenly cooked. This will take approximately 3 hours.

When the quinces are tender and breaking down, purée the fruit along with any liquid in a jug blender and pass through a fine sieve. Place 4–5 clean jars on a baking sheet and put them into a cool oven, 120°C/gas mark ½.

Weigh the pulp. This recipe should yield approximately 1.9kg. Weigh out the same amount of sugar, return both ingredients to the pan and stir over a low heat to dissolve the sugar. It is faster to finish the pulp in two batches, so remove half to a large bowl and continue to cook the portion that remains in the pan. Turn the heat up to medium and cook, stirring constantly with a heatproof spatula or flat wooden spoon, until a rapid boil is achieved. Then reduce the heat to low and continue to stir until the mixture thickens and a spoon drawn across the bottom leaves a clean trail, approx 15–20 minutes.

Pot the first batch of cheese into the sterilised jars and then finish the second batch. Cover the surface of the quince cheese with a waxed-paper disc and seal the jar with cellophane. Store in a cool, dark place and use within 1 year.

# QUINCE JELLY

✳ Makes about 1.6kg – 3 or 4 jars ✳ Preparation time 30 minutes ✳ Cooking time 4 hours spread over 2 days

This delicate, amber-coloured preserve can be served with terrines (see page 57) or game pies, but it is also very nice in apple pies. Japonica quinces are small, very hard fruits from decorative trees and can be used in combination with, or as opposed to, the pear quinces.

**1½kg pear or Japonica quinces**

**approx 750g jam sugar**

special equipment

**a stainless steel preserving pan, a jelly bag or muslin and a sugar thermometer or temperature probe**

If you are using pear quinces, rub off any fur. Wash and chop the fruit into small pieces, including the peel and cores. Discard any black or brown pieces.

Place the quinces in a stainless steel pan, cover with water and bring to the boil, then turn the heat to low and simmer until the fruit is completely soft, topping up the water as necessary to ensure the fruit is always just covered. This will take 2–3 hours. Stir occasionally to ensure that the fruit is not catching on the bottom of the pan. Once cooked, strain the hot liquid carefully through a jelly bag or muslin-lined sieve. Do not squeeze or press the pulp through, or the jelly will turn cloudy. It can be left to drip overnight.

When you are ready to finish the jelly, heat the oven to 120°C/ gas mark ½ and place your clean jars in the oven on a baking sheet. At the same time, place a couple of saucers in the fridge. Discard the pulp and measure the liquid (you should have around 1 litre). Return this to the cleaned pan over a medium heat. For every litre of liquid, add 750g jam sugar to the pan and stir to dissolve.

Bring the mixture to a rapid boil, stirring regularly to prevent sticking. Keep at a rolling boil until setting point is reached. Once the jelly mixture reaches about 105°C and begins to thicken, test for setting point using the cold-saucer method on page 74. Once this has been reached, remove the pan from the heat and allow the jelly to sit for a minute to form a skin. Remove and discard any scum that has formed and pot the jelly into the sterilised jars. Cover the surface of the jelly with a waxed-paper disc and seal each jar with cellophane.

# PLUM JELLY

✱ Makes approx 1.8kg – 4 or 5 jars  ✱ Preparation time 1 hour 30 minutes over 2 days

✱ Cooking time 15 minutes

Mrs Beeton used either damsons or greengages for most of her plum preserves.
Each plum has a distinct flavour, so choose the ones you like the most. You can gather
cherry plums from old hedgerows in late July and early August. Whichever plum you use,
the result is a clear, brilliant, tart jelly that is lovely eaten with a fresh cream cheese or
served with game dishes in the winter as an alternative to redcurrant jelly.

**1.5kg cherry plums or
other small plums, stalks
removed**

**approx 900g jam sugar**

special equipment

**a stainless steel preserving
pan, a jelly bag or muslin and
a sugar thermometer or
temperature probe**

Place the washed plums in a stainless steel pan with 600ml
water. Cook over a medium heat until the juices run and the
fruit breaks down completely. Strain the hot, cooked plums
through a jelly bag or muslin-lined sieve over a large bowl,
and leave to drip overnight.

When you are ready to finish the jelly, place your clean jars
on a baking sheet in a cool oven, 120°C/gas mark ½. Place a
couple of saucers in the fridge for testing the set. Measure the
juice: allow 750g jam sugar for each litre of liquid. This recipe
should yield about 1.2 litres juice, which would require 900g
of jam sugar. Place the juice and sugar in a clean stainless
steel pan. Dissolve the sugar first over a low heat, stirring
frequently to prevent sticking, then bring the jelly to a rolling
boil and cook until it reaches a temperature of 105°C.

When the mixture begins to thicken, start testing for setting
point using the cold-saucer method on page 74. When it is
ready, remove from the heat and allow the jam to form a skin.

Remove and discard any scum that has formed, then pot the
jam into the warm, sterilised jars. Cover the surface of the jelly
with a waxed-paper disc and seal the jar with cellophane.

# BREAD SAUCE

✳ Serves 4 ✳ Preparation time 10 minutes ✳ Cooking time 1 hour including 30 minutes infusing time

Either milk or stock can be used for this sauce, though milk gives a creamier result. This sauce has the classic milk seasonings of pepper, mace and bay to add piquancy. As Mrs Beeton says, it should be used alongside game or poultry.

500ml whole milk

1 small onion, peeled and quartered

1 bay leaf

½ tsp black peppercorns

3 cloves

2 blades mace

100g stale white breadcrumbs

15g butter

20ml double cream

grated nutmeg, to taste

salt and freshly ground black pepper

Place the milk, onion, bay leaf, peppercorns, cloves, and mace and a few gratings of nutmeg in a saucepan over a medium heat. Bring the mixture to simmering then remove from the heat. Cover with a lid and leave for 30 minutes to infuse.

Strain the milk through a fine sieve into a clean pan set on a low heat, discarding the vegetables and whole spices. Add the breadcrumbs and cook gently, stirring occasionally for 10–15 minutes, or until the sauce is very thick but still soft and smooth. Beat in the butter and cream, and season the sauce with about ¼ tsp each salt and black pepper. Transfer to a warmed gravy boat or serving jug, cover and rest for 15–20 minutes in a warm place. Grate a little nutmeg over, beat it in and serve.

# PARSLEY & GARLIC BUTTER

✳ Makes 100g ✳ Preparation time 5 minutes

Mrs Beeton's parsley butter was suggested as an accompaniment to boiled fowls – which we rarely cook today. However, the addition of a little garlic turns the original recipe into a versatile butter for the modern kitchen. It is whipped to ensure that it does not run when heated.

100g softened unsalted butter

large bunch of parsley, leaves only, finely chopped

2 garlic cloves, finely chopped

½ tsp Maldon or other flaky salt

Place the butter in a medium-sized bowl and whip until creamy, pale and fluffy. Add the parsley, garlic and salt and whip until combined.

Cover and chill until required. It will keep for 2 days in the fridge.

# RASPBERRY VINEGAR

✳ Makes approx 2 litres ✳ Preparation time 10 minutes over 3 days

Mrs Beeton used raspberry vinegar diluted with water as a tonic. In fact, because it is so intensely fruity, it also makes a super addition to dressings or to game dishes. Try using a splash when cooking liver – it is a delicious combination.

1.5kg raspberries

1kg caster sugar

1 litre white wine vinegar or cider vinegar

special equipment

a large stainless steel or ceramic bowl and a jelly bag or muslin

Place the raspberries in a large stainless steel or ceramic bowl and crush lightly. Add the sugar and the vinegar and cover. Steep together for 3 days and then strain the vinegar through a colander lined with muslin suspended over a large bowl. Alternatively, use a jelly bag and stand. Transfer the vinegar into vinegar bottles that have non-reactive seals. Store in a cool, dark place for at least 1 month, and then use within 1 year.

# CHESTNUT FORCEMEAT

✳ Serves 8 ✳ Preparation time 15 minutes ✳ Cooking time 1 hour 15 minutes

Forcemeat is often a combination of cooked and raw meat, flavoured with herbs or lemon, and traditionally baked and used as a stuffing. It was very popular at the time Mrs Beeton was writing, and she included several recipes for it in her book. The addition of chestnuts and apples here gives the forcemeat both texture and a light acidity. Make it to accompany your roast goose or turkey.

500g fresh white breadcrumbs

500g chestnuts, boiled, skinned and roughly chopped

500g sausage meat or skinned sausages

2 large onions, peeled and roughly chopped

200g chopped ready-to-eat prunes

large bunch thyme, leaves only, stems discarded

6 sage leaves, finely chopped

100g suet, grated

½ tsp freshly ground black pepper

75ml white wine

75ml dark chicken stock (see page 67)

1 tsp salt

500g cooking apples, peeled, cored and chopped

50g softened butter

special equipment

a ceramic or metal roasting tin or a pie dish

Combine all the ingredients in a large bowl and squeeze them together with your hands to amalgamate. Now proceed one of two ways.

The first option is to preheat the oven to 180°C/gas mark 5, press everything into a ceramic or metal roasting tin and smooth the surface. Bake for 45 minutes, until lightly browned, then stir up the mixture to break it up, and press down again. Bake for another 30 minutes, or until browned well and crisp on top.

The second method is to preheat the oven to 200°C/gas mark 6. Form the forcemeat into golf ball-sized balls and place them snugly into a pie dish. Bake for 20 minutes.

Serve with roast goose or turkey.

> 'The exercise or diversion of pursuing four-footed beasts of game is called
> hunting, which, to this day, is followed in the field and the forest, with gun
> and greyhound. Birds, on the contrary, are not hunted, but shot in the air, or
> taken with nets and other devices, which is called fowling.'
>
> *Beeton's Book of Household Management*

# FAIR GAME

In the 19th century, conservation was not high on the agenda and gaming was 'in many instances ... carried to an excess'. Mrs Beeton records the extraordinary exploits of the king of Naples who, on a hunting expedition 'pursued during his journey to Vienna, in Austria, Bohemia, and Moravia ... killed 5 bears, 1,820 boars, 1,950 deer, 1,145 does, 1,625 roebucks, 11,121 rabbits, 13 wolves, 17 badgers, 16,354 hares, and 354 foxes. In birds, during the same expedition, he killed 15,350 pheasants and 12,335 partridges.

'Such an amount of destruction can hardly be called sport', Isabella noted; 'it resembles more the indiscriminate slaughter of a battlefield, where the scientific engines of civilised warfare are brought to bear upon defenceless savages.'

The laws concerning the shooting and sale of game have thankfully changed a great deal in the last 150 years, and the Code of Good Shooting Practice helps ensure sustainable shooting, with its stipulation that shot game 'is food and must be treated as such'. Today, over a million people are involved in shooting in the UK, and many more of us enjoy eating the end product as consumers of pheasants, partridges and other game.

A large, formal driven-game shoot is still likely to have far more birds shot down than its paying guests will want to take home for their own use. But both the Game Conservancy Trust and the British Association for Shooting and Conservation have put pressure on sporting estates to find markets for the birds, with shoot managers encouraged to sell the excess on to game dealers, supermarkets or directly to the public, even if the distribution process actually loses the shoot money.

There are a number of game birds, waterfowl (ducks, geese and waders) and other bird species, as well as mammals, which can be shot legally. The charts overleaf give the seasons for each.

# DEER SEASON

| Red deer | Stag | 1 August – 30 April in England and Wales<br>1 July – 20 October in Scotland<br>1 August – 30 April in Northern Ireland |
| --- | --- | --- |
| | Hind | 1 November – 31 March in England and Wales<br>21 October – 15 February in Scotland<br>1 November – 28/29 February in Northern Ireland |
| Fallow deer | Buck | 1 August – 30 April in England and Wales<br>1 August – 30 April in Scotland<br>1 August – 30 April in Northern Ireland |
| | Doe | 1 November – 31 March in England and Wales<br>21 October – 15 February in Scotland<br>1 November – 28/29 February in Northern Ireland |
| Sika deer | Stag | 1 August – 30 April in England and Wales<br>1 July – 20 October in Scotland<br>1 August – 30 April in Northern Ireland |
| | Hind | 1 November – 31 March in England and Wales<br>21 October – 15 February in Scotland<br>1 November – 28/29 February in Northern Ireland |
| Roe deer | Buck | 1 April – 31 October in England and Wales<br>1 April – 20 October in Scotland |
| | Doe | 1 November – 31 March in England and Wales<br>21 October – 31 March in Scotland |

# GAMEBIRDS & WATERFOWL

Pheasant

1 October – 1 February in England, Wales and Scotland
1 October – 31 January in Northern Ireland

Grey partridge

1 September – 1 February in England, Wales and Scotland
1 September – 31 January in Northern Ireland

Red-legged partridge

1 September – 1 February in England, Wales and Scotland
1 September – 31 January in Northern Ireland

Red grouse

12 August – 10 December in England, Wales and Scotland
12 August – 30 November in Northern Ireland

Duck and goose

1 September – 31 January in England, Wales and Scotland
1 September – 31 January in Northern Ireland

Common snipe

12 August – 31 January in England, Wales and Scotland
1 September – 31 January in Northern Ireland

Woodcock

1 October – 31 January in England, Northern Ireland and Wales
1 September – 31 January in Scotland

Wood pigeon

No close season in England, Wales, Scotland and Northern
Ireland subject to complying with the terms and conditions
of the relevant game licence

# GROUND GAME

Brown mountain hare

1 January – 31 December in England, Wales and Scotland
on moorland and unenclosed land

12 August – 31 January in Northern Ireland

Rabbit

1 January – 31 December in England, Wales and Scotland
on moorland and unenclosed land

No close season in Northern Ireland

# FREE RANGE

In recent years, the wide availability of chickens and turkeys raised in factory-like conditions has turned what was once highly prized meat into something cheap and largely flavourless, not to mention what it has done to the quality of life of the animals. Free-range or organic poultry, which is more likely to be produced on a smaller scale and from a variety of breeds, is much more likely to taste authentic. Among fowl, British geese are almost always free-range or organic.

## Indoor-reared

Most birds produced in the UK are reared indoors. They are densely stocked, with up to 15–16 mature birds per square metre. Additionally, they are bred to mature very quickly, reaching full size in 6–7 weeks. This results in a cheaper chicken, but it has little flavour. Indoor-reared chickens that bear the RSPCA's Freedom Food logo are still produced in large flocks in closed-barn systems, but they are kept at a slightly lower density, and allowed some natural light.

## Free range

A growing number of large-scale producers use free-range systems, but these are not always as you might imagine. Many of the larger free-range systems are essentially barn systems with small exits that allow (but do not encourage) birds outside. Smaller free-range producers usually have more open systems in which birds do roam freely out-of-doors. However, these only account for a small percentage of the free-range poultry available in the shops.

## Organic

Organic chickens are reared in smaller flocks than those in the other systems – under Soil Association rules, there must be no more than 1000 birds per flock. Producers are also encouraged to use traditional breeds that grow and mature at a natural rate. The longer growing time means that organic birds are more expensive to produce, and the cost must be passed on to the consumer, but the chickens are generally of superb flavour. Organic chickens also do not have their movements restricted like caged birds and are more likely to be produced in good conditions with more access to the open air than even free-range birds. For those concerned with animal welfare, an organic bird is the best option.

# PRODUCERS & SUPPLIERS

## Meat

### The Blackface Meat Company

Weatherall Foods Limited,
Crochmore House,
Irongray, Dumfries DG2 9SF

Tel 01387 730 326

www.blackface.co.uk

This small family business rears Blackface sheep and
Galloway cattle in the south west of Scotland. Their
superb mutton, lamb, game, beef and pork is
produced with care and attention.

### Fletchers Reediehill Deer Farm

Auchtermuchty, Fife KY14 7HS

Tel 01337 828 369

www.seriouslygoodvenison.co.uk

Nicola and John Fletcher are experts in producing
farmed Red deer. Their meat is reared to exceptionally
high standards and tastes delicious.

### Graig Farm

Dolau,
Llandrindod Wells,
Powys LD1 5TL

Tel 01686 627 979

www.graigfarm.co.uk

This farm supplies a wide range of organic products,
including meat and poultry, from its online shop. All of
their produce is cared for to high standards.

### Peele's Norfolk Black Turkeys

Rookery Farm, Thuxton, Norwich,
Norfolk NR9 4QJ

Tel 01362 850 237

www.peelesblackturkeys.co.uk

A producer of Norfolk Black turkeys for four generations.
The birds are reared outside and allowed to mature
slowly on a diet of home-grown wheat, barley, oats and
beans. Their flavour is unlike any other bird and tastes
like turkey should.

### Rhug Estate

Corwen, Denbighshire LL21 0EH

Tel 01490 413 000

www.rhug.co.uk

An organic farm and butchery supplying a variety of
meat including Aberdeen Angus beef, Salt Marsh lamb,
chicken, game and traditional Duroc pork. All the meat
(with the exception of the game, which is sourced as
locally as possible) is organic and comes from their
own farms.

### St Brides Farm

High Kype Road, Sandford,
Strathaven ML10 6PRT

Tel 01357 529 989

www.stbridespoultry.co.uk

Free range chickens and ducks are produced on this
small poultry farm just outside of Strathaven, favouring
slower growing, flavourful breeds which naturally thrive
in the free-range setting.

## Spices

### Green Saffron Spices

Unit 16, Knockgriffin,
Midleton, Cork, Ireland

Tel 00 353 21 463 7960

www.greensaffron.com

Arun and Olive Kapil's family business imports and
grinds premium spices from family farms across India.

## Equipment

### Lakeland

Alexandra Buildings, Windermere,
Cumbria LA23 1BQ

Tel 01539 488 100

www.lakeland.co.uk

Lakeland provides an array of innovative cookware,
appliances and utensils. The company places enormous
value on customer satisfaction, and uses customer
feedback to develop its vast range.

## Nisbets Catering Equipment

Fourth Way, Avonmouth,
Bristol BS11 8TB

Tel 0845 140 5555

www.nisbets.co.uk

This is one of the UK's largest suppliers of catering equipment, and a great source of larger scale cooking equipment such as stock pots.

## Useful organisations

### The British Association for Shooting and Conservation

Marford Mill, Rossett,
Wrexham, LL12 0HL

Tel 01244 573 000

www.basc.org.uk

BASC promote and protect sporting shooting of all types throughout the UK, and produce Codes of Practice detailing the law surrounding shooting game.

### FARMA

Lower Ground Floor, 12 Southgate Street,
Winchester, Hampshire SO23 9EF

Tel 0845 458 8420

www.farmersmarkets.net

The National Farmers' Retail & Markets Association represents the sale of local food and fresh farm products direct to the public through farmers' markets and farm shops. Visit their website for a list of certified markets and suppliers in your area.

### Freedom Food Limited

Wilberforce Way,
Southwater, Horsham,
West Sussex RH139RS

Tel 0300 123 0014

www.rspca.org.uk/freedomfood

Freedom Food is the RSPCA's farm assurance and food labelling scheme. It is the only UK farm assurance scheme to focus solely on improving the welfare of farm animals reared for food.

### Game and Wildlife Conservation Trust

Burgate Manor, Fordingbridge
Hampshire, SP6 1EF

www.gwct.org.uk

The Game and Wildlife Conservation Trust is a charity that researches and develops game and wildlife management techniques, providing training and advice to farmers, gamekeepers and land managers on how best to improve the biodiversity of the countryside.

### Rare Breeds Survival Trust

Stoneleigh Park,
Nr Kenilworth,
Warwickshire CV8 2LG

Tel 024 7669 6551

www.rbst.org.uk

The Rare Breeds Survival Trust is a charity that is concerned with conserving Britain's native farm livestock. Contact them for lists of rare breed suppliers and producers in your area.

### Slow Food UK

Slow Food UK, 6 Neal's Yard, Covent Garden,
London WC2H 9DP

Tel 020 7099 1132

www.slowfood.org.uk

Slow Food UK is part of the global Slow Food movement. It has thousands of members and connections with local groups around the UK that link the pleasure of artisan food to community and the environment.

### Soil Association

South Plaza,
Marlborough Street,
Bristol BS1 3NX
Tel 0117 314 5000

www.soilassociation.org

The Soil Association is a charity campaigning for planet-friendly food and farming. It offers guidance to consumers looking for local suppliers of organic food as well as advice for organic growers and businesses.

# GLOSSARY OF COOKING TERMS

Many languages have influenced the British kitchen, but none so much as French – hardly surprising surprising since French food has often been held up as the benchmark for excellence, in Mrs Beeton's time as well as in our own. Long before the Michelin guide began to report on British restaurants, French chefs were working for British royalty and could be found in the kitchens of many large country houses. Perhaps the most famous of these was Antonin Carême, chef to the Prince Regent (later George IV), who set the standard for future chefs to emulate. Mrs Beeton knew of him by name and reputation. The list below is intended to help explain the more commonly used terms – many, but not all, of which come from the French.

**arrowroot**   a powdered starch made from the roots of a tropical plant. It is used to thicken sauces, giving a lovely transparent result

**baste**   to moisten meat or poultry during the roasting process by pouring over fat or liquid

**beat**   to mix food energetically to introduce air, using a wooden spoon, whisk or electric mixer to make a mixture light and fluffy

**beurre manié**   a paste made from butter and flour that is used to thicken hot sauces

**blender**   a machine used for blending or puréeing, particularly in the preparation of soups and sauces. It can be in the form of a jug into which liquids are poured, or hand held (known as a wand or stick blender) for use in a bowl or saucepan

**boil**   to heat a liquid to the point at which it bubbles vigorously and begins to vapourise – 100°C in the case of water

**bone**   to remove the bones from fish, meat or poultry

**braise**   to cook slowly in a covered pan or dish, with liquid

**brine**   a saltwater solution used for preserving and pickling

**brown**   to colour the surface of a food by cooking it in hot fat, caramelising the sugars and developing flavour

**casserole**   a deep, lidded cooking pot made from an ovenproof material

**chill**   to cool food without freezing, usually in a refrigerator

**chine**   to separate the backbone from the ribs in a joint of meat, to make carving easier

**chinois**   a conical sieve with a very fine mesh used for straining soups, sauces and purées to give a very smooth result

**clarify**   (of stock) to remove sediment or filter using egg white (see page 64)

**colander**   metal or plastic basket used for draining food such as cooked vegetables

**cornflour**   the ground kernels of corn/maize, used for thickening liquids and sauces

**de-glaze**   to add liquid to a pan after roasting or sautéeing in order to dissolve any juices or sediment left in the base of the pan, picking up their flavour

**devil**   to cook with spicy seasoning

**dice**   to cut food into small cubes

**dress**   to prepare poultry, game or shellfish

**dripping**   the fat which drips from meat, poultry or game during cooking

**flambé or flame**   to remove the alcohol from hot food by lighting the fumes

**flameproof**   describes cookware or utensils which can be used with direct heat or in a hot oven

**forcemeat**   a seasoned mixture of breadcrumbs or meat and vegetables, often used to stuff birds before cooking. Now more commonly known in this context as stuffing

**freeze**   to preserve food by chilling and storing well below 0°C

**fricassee**   a stew, usually of chicken or veal

**game**   wild or wild-reared birds or mammals, shot within a restricted season (see page 89)

**giblets**   the neck, gizzard, liver and heart of poultry or game

**gravy**   a sauce made from the juices exuded from meat, poultry or game during cooking, combined with stock or water and starch

**hang**   to suspend meat or game in a cool, dry place until matured and tenderised

**joint**   to cut an animal or piece of meat into smaller pieces by cutting through the joints to separate the bones. Also a piece of meat for roasting

**jugged**   (of game) cooked in a covered pot, usually with blood added for gravy; (of kippers) cooked in a jug

**leveret**   a hare aged up to 1 year old

**par-boil**   to part cook in water

**pickle**   to preserve meat or vegetables in brine or vinegar

**reduce**   to concentrate a liquid, for example a sauce or stock, by boiling it until a portion has evaporated

**roast**   to cook in the oven or on a spit over an open flame

**sear**   to brown meat rapidly using a fierce heat to seal in the juices

**seasoned flour**   flour mixed with salt and pepper, and sometimes other spices, often used to coat meat or fish before cooking

**sediment**   a solid residue left in the bottom of a tin after roasting meat or poultry

**skillet**   a heavy cast iron frying pan

**skim**   to remove residue from the surface of a liquid, for example fat from stock or scum from jam

**steep**   to soak in liquid, in order to hydrate

**stew**   to simmer food slowly in a casserole or covered pan

**terrine**   an earthenware pot used to make and serve pâté. Also its contents

**truss**   to tie a bird or piece of meat into a neat shape using string

**venison**   the meat from deer

# INDEX

# ACKNOWLEDGEMENTS

Mum, Sandra Baker, helped without question in the kitchen and office both in the process of testing the recipes and in organising manuscripts – you are a blessing.

To my sister Louise, and to Oscar and Fanny for providing moral support go hearty thanks. Much respect and love goes to Dad, John Baker, for being such a lover of shooting and game who has provided us with a wonderful supply of delicious food for so many years.

Had I not worked with Joyce Molyneux, I would probably never have known that game could reach such heights. Her kitchen was a marvellous place, and no one else I know loves game quite like her. Adam Sellar provided great support in the kitchen during the testing of the recipes – thank you.

Amanda Harris and Debbie Woska sat through the creation of *Mrs Beeton How to Cook* with me – providing just the right amount of support and encouragement – thank you. Zelda Turner deserves thanks for helping trim and sculpt the recipes in this smaller collection. To all the design team – Julyan Bayes, Lucie Steriker, Sammy-Jo Squire and her crew, and the photographer Andrew Hayes-Watkins and his team for making the book look so beautiful. The team behind the scenes at Orion helped enormously – Elizabeth Allen and Nicky Carswell especially.

Suppliers and helpers were many – but chiefly thanks go to Mike Wilson and his team in Patrington for supplying me with poultry and game in quantity for so many years. Finally, thanks to my friend Piffa Schroder – the best shot, and also Natasha and Will Ramsey who deserve huge thanks for being such supportive friends in the dining room at Chesthill.

Gerard Baker